How to Hide
Almost Anything

How to Hide Almost Anything

by DAVID KROTZ

Illustrated by Nina Sklansky

WILLIAM MORROW & COMPANY, INC., NEW YORK   1975

Printed in the United States of America.

1 2 3 4 5 79 78 77 76 75

Library of Congress Cataloging in Publication Data

Krotz, David.
  How to hide almost anything.

    1. Hiding-places (Secret chambers, etc.) 2. Wood-
work. I. Title.
TT200.K76   643   74-30320
ISBN 0-688-02894-2

Book design by Helen Roberts

For Joanna

I will take you yet to hazel fields.
I will hold you in my side.
As the moon-ripe fruit hangs before our eyes,
We shall share our feasts,
We shall love and share our shields,
We shall lie together.

Contents

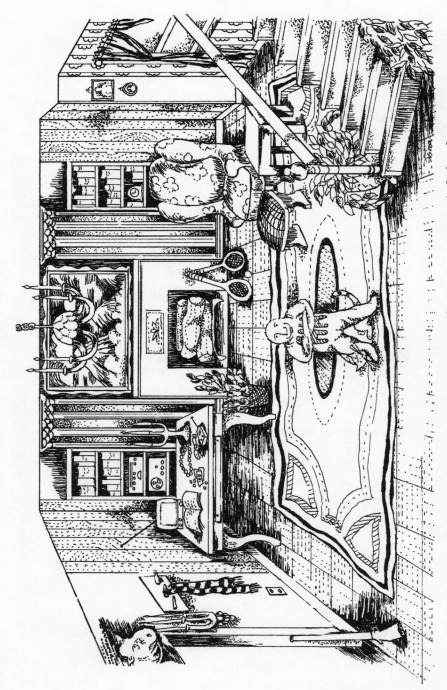

There are 17 secret compartments in this room—can you find them?
(SEE SPECIAL APPENDIX TO FIND OUT)

Introduction: The Story of Something to Hide?

IT ALL BEGAN WITH POVERTY. MY WIFE CAME IN from the winter cold, clenching the morning bills in her hands, and I sat smoking cigarettes to the ends wondering how we were going to pay to keep that warm apartment around us. Outside the frosted glass, the weird and the gifted people of New York's Greenwich Village wandered the angled streets; it was still the charming artists' quarter, but I didn't find my life there charming at the moment. For while the President's haggard face spoke optimistic words on the tube, the economy got worse and worse—and I was out of work.

I'd knocked around a lot of jobs during my twenty-eight years trying to pay for a writing habit. Low-pay jobs, stopgap work: like many of my generation, I was always in transition. But I was getting hungry for a little lucre. It was time the good life came my way. And what that meant was money, healthy income.

I was on my way to the employment agency when the lucky idea fell into my head. As I prepared to leave the apartment there was a ritual to be followed. Going out in New York can be an involved task, especially if you live on the first floor in a neighborhood frequented by burglars and other rogues. My previous apartment had been sacked, and I lost camera, radio, guitar, and stereo. With the window open and the apartment empty, I was left shamefaced and furious.

Since that time I'd moved to a better neighborhood and had taken precautions against such a recurrence. Consequently, as I prepared to leave, I turned on lights to give the appearance I was home and dialed dreamy music on the radio. While sinking three-and-a-half-inch security screws into the predrilled holes of the windows, my mind once again mulled over the ever-present possibility—*what would they get if they broke in tonight?* If I only had some way to hide my valuables. Then suddenly—*a secret hiding place.* I could build one!

Having worked as a carpenter and house painter in the past, I had the basic skills. But actually, skill was less important than ingenuity. I thought of all the apartments being broken into in Manhattan at exactly that moment; doors being literally smashed on the Upper West Side; violent entrance through fire-escape windows on the Lower East Side; picked locks in posh apartments of the Upper East Side; and right here in Greenwich Village, the junkies were moving in, burglaries and mean muggings following in their wake. If I could build one secret hiding place, why couldn't I build more? Why couldn't I start a business conceiving and creating hidey holes? Thoughts raced furiously now. *The contemporary art form . . . personalized hiding places. In modern society more than ever before, everyone has something to hide: jewels, money, appliances, grass, pornography, whips. Here, let me help you.* Suddenly the name for the business came . . . SOMETHING TO HIDE? Techniques and locations began to flash before my glazed eyes: locking devices, ruses, subterfuge. With all this preconceived intrigue, I felt like a video detective setting out toward his guaranteed happy ending.

I mulled the idea. *A hidey hole in every home. Let me give you that extra space you always wanted. I can hide anything.* Though sneaky ideas engorged my cranium, I couldn't afford to lay out much money. I needed an advertising gimmick. Who could afford big newspaper ads for a business that might never get off the ground? There had to be another approach. What if I printed up business cards first. I could write a jazzy one-page sales pitch and mimeograph it, then stand on the street with a sign on my back, hat pulled down over my eyes, passing out literature.

The notion carried. This is the wording I finally decided upon for the sign.

SOMETHING TO HIDE?

We custom build in
Your domicile
Secret places
Ask for my card

Note the royal "We." The business cards weren't to be ready for a week so I placed a two-line ad to run in the *Village Voice,* a weekly newspaper. I needed some feedback to find out if the idea would really work. Then I set about getting my tools in order. I was lacking chisels, a good brace, and bit. Countless other items came to mind convincing me I could easily blow a hundred dollars on tools alone. Better to start with basics. That and muscle was all that was really needed. Speed and finesse could come later.

The day for the *Village Voice* arrived. I ran out to buy it. Eyes scanned once, twice, no ad. I got quick satisfaction for their error, and they agreed to run the ad for two weeks in reparation.

In the meantime, the business cards, the mimeographed sales pitch, and the sign were done. It was time to go out on the street. With the sign draped in a sheet under my arm, I sidled around looking for a likely street corner to set myself upon. I felt like a hooker, of dubious charms.

I was an instant success as far as the throngs were concerned. Another Greenwich Village weirdo, something to gawk at and chortle about. I was very uncomfortable standing there, my two-foot-by-four-foot sign questioning the staring eyes in three colors, SOMETHING TO HIDE? They laughed, and I got red in the face as I shifted from foot to foot. Then someone came up and asked for my card. Because he broke the ice and approached me, a man who had been hanging back and watching also came up and nervously asked. Smiling now, I handed both of them my spare-worded business card, taped to the folded sales pitch, which read:

SOMETHING TO HIDE?

New York (phone number)
We discreetly build, in your house or apartment, secret places and hidey holes which are both integral in the existing struc-

ture and detection-proof from searching intruders. Each new job is a challenge to our artistically honed and intrigue-trained minds. We discuss your wants, and size and accessibility of the secret place—be it a closetlike space or more common cache-sized hole—and then set to finding the most suitable location in your domicile. Our imaginations are fertile and we utilize our craftsmanship as proudly as we employ our skilled secrets to help you achieve that extra space of privacy. In combination, the services we offer are unique. We descend from and draw upon a heritage of need; the king, the insurgent, the libertine, and the most staid judge—those with something to safeguard have long called upon specialists like ourselves. Our minimum charge which includes all materials and labor is one hundred dollars. We have found most jobs don't necessitate a larger fee. Call us for a casual appointment and estimate.

The two prospective customers wandered off reading my materials, and I was left alone again, waiting. The initial flush of nervousness and exhilaration was gone, and the cold air began to penetrate my jacket. It was obvious that this job would require long underwear and short stints on the street. Taking a paperback book out of my pocket, I leaned my hands on a parking meter and began to read.

In an hour and forty-five minutes, I passed out ten requested cards. About one every ten minutes. Half of the people were over thirty and very prosperous-looking. That's where the money was.

Waiting for the *Village Voice* to finally print the ad, waiting for that first phone call and first job, I went to New York's Forty-second Street library and started researching my new profession. I, of course, grew up watching the same movies as everyone else, the ones with secret passages in the castle, the hidden compartments in the study, bookcases that miraculously slide open. Despite the fact that most of this was pure Hollywood Hogwash, I was convinced that there must be some heritage involved in the secret-compartment idea. I had ad-libbed on that theme in my sales brochure, trying to strike a responsive chord in my customers' romantic souls. I came away from the library with little return for my effort; no one seemed to have written a book on building secret compartments.

But the idea was good. I was convinced. Most American homes are hollow anyway, hollow with cheap materials and careless craftsmanship. Why not refine some of that space into something unique and serviceable? Secret compartments that reflect the character and the needs of the public. I was willing to offer my imagination; all America needed was money. One thing I was dead set on avoiding, however, was the cliché and obvious hiding place: the-wall-safe-behind-the-picture sort of thing. I planned on making good on my word, because I knew I could do it—nondetectable secret space. Of course, no construction could be safe from a wielded sledgehammer or the X-ray eyes of modern technology, but I was staking my nonexistent reputation on the fact that I could make compartments that eagle-eyed burglars and sniffing police couldn't find.

I stood on the street again the next day and that night too.

The first call came. It was a man in Brooklyn who had visited the Village with his girl friend the night before. He wanted me to come to his newly purchased house and give him an estimate on what I could do for him.

I rode a subway to Brooklyn for the appointment, checking myself to see if I had everything: tape measure, pencil and pad, confident expression, and a pat story about how I'd been doing this more than a month for completely satisfied customers.

The guy was a thirtyish black man who ran a record store in midtown Manhattan. The house he'd bought was fifty years old, wood, and he was having the unfinished basement done over into an apartment for himself, planning on renting out the top floors. While I looked around, I asked him how much space he needed hidden and then I saw the perfect location. Beside the brick fireplace was a two-foot-by-one-foot cubbyhole inset, and it ran from floor to ceiling. It would be simple to put a false wall in front of that and make it become part of the room's normal wall line. I retired to a corner to jot sketches. The problem was, of course, how to gain entrance and still have it appear a solid wall. I have to admit I didn't come to any snap solutions on that one. I dickered with this idea and that, and the man began to get impatient, but I held him off with, "I'm trying to decide whether I can give you my best entrance for your price range."

I was about to go ahead and give an estimate and leave the figuring out to later when the idea of wall paneling occurred to me (see Chapters 2 and 4). It proved the perfect solution. I swaggered back to the customer, explained in general terms (because I couldn't give too much away before getting paid) what I would do and how much it would cost, two hundred dollars. He found it a bit steep but finally agreed. I came back the following day and completed the job in six hours. The business was off to a start. My cheeks were rosy as I walked home in the cold night with money in my pocket.

The *Voice* ad finally appeared and almost immediately a call came from the "Scenes" columnist of that paper. It was an offbeat column that did short pieces on far-ranging topics. I was invited into her office for an interview. By this time I had picked up another job, a small, cache-sized hole which I opted to do between wall studs (see Chapter 2). The interview went marvelously, possibly because I was really beginning to feel justified in my enthusiasm for the scheme. Hamming it up a bit I gave her a few quotable lines, ". . . David doesn't use his last name because of what he terms 'the often discreet nature of his work.'"

I picked up a couple more jobs from the *Voice* ad and my street-standing as I waited to see the effect of the publicity in "Scenes." I hadn't begun to hope for what ensued. The phone started ringing the first day the column appeared, and I was scheduling free estimates left and center. Not all of these worked out to jobs, obviously, but from that point on I had as much work as I wanted to handle. And there was another offshoot from the debut in the "Scenes" column—more media interest.

I got a call and a subsequent visit from a charming woman who worked for National Radio Broadcasting, an outfit that did human interest interviews which were syndicated to over a hundred radio stations across the country, including WNYC in New York. She came to my apartment with a huge tape recorder. I offered her brandy, and with the wheels of tape turning, she asked questions and I talked. When the interview finally was aired on WNYC, I had my own tape machine ready to record it for posterity and was surprised to hear they had dubbed in a man asking me the questions, and the woman I met was nowhere to be heard. Such is the fate of women, still.

Yet one more odd connection was made through that "Scenes" column: Weeks later, a German-accented free-lance writer called. I gave him my speech, always being careful not to betray my customers' confidences, or to reveal too much about the operation for fear of competition. He convinced me to do a mockup of a "typical hidey hole" so he could shoot some before-and-after pictures. He also arranged to shoot a roll of film of me and my sign on the corner of Seventy-second Street and Broadway. His article and two photos subsequently appeared in *The National Enquirer*.

As I gained experience I learned to handle anything that came up. To earn money, I had to spend it, but the profit margin was large and suddenly I found myself living well. The publicity had got me off the ground and started the first flood of jobs coming in. After that, I benefited by referrals from satisfied customers. I hung a little addendum to the sign on my back that cataloged my media exposure, and the street still proved a viable way of bringing in jobs.

There were a lot of problems connected with the work. Using a car in New York City to carry materials and then having to worry about twenty-five-dollar parking tickets or the exorbitant cost of parking in garages. There were people who didn't pay their bills, though I always pushed for cash. Night hours were usually required and that was a problem. After a while, I have to admit, I began to get bored. Once I had conceived the basic designs, the fun seemed to go out of it. I liked finding the best location in an apartment and designing the secret access to the construct, but repetitive building wasn't nearly as satisfying. I have retired now from active secret building, but there is no reason you can't begin.

As you can imagine, the notion of hiding things is not new—probably as old as man himself. I suspect it all began with a cavewoman taking a piece of meat wrapped in leaves and hiding it away from some insatiable beast-hubby so the kids would have something to eat in the morning. Unfortunately, what we can learn from the past masters of concealment is limited. This book is my personal treasury. It will show you some of the designs and ideas I've used, as well as other sneakies I never got around to building. It's a book of concrete information and approaches as well as a primer in the concepts of SeComp (Secret Compartment) design.

For those merely seeking pragmatic object safety I think

you'll find more here than you need to know to secrete what you value. Fortunately, the spirit of '76 still lives in some hearts out there, stout defenders to the end against intrusions external and domestic. Those spirits will seize this chance to safeguard a patch of territory, a small victory against encroaching corruption, a secret respository for wealth, possessions, or highs.

This is a modest product of my experiences. It is a useful tool to anyone who knows the rudiments of carpentry. Total neophytes can read the section titled "Carpentry" in Special Appendix. You can do it if you try. You can build that extra space of privacy for yourself. Here are many designs and models. They can be easily duplicated or used as inspiration for wholly new conceptions. Much of what you read in the early part of the book will be helpful in the latter part. It is a chronological acquaintanceship. So, come along, join the tradition of those kings, insurgents, libertines, and judges. Everyone should have a hidey hole in his or her home. Everyone has *something* to hide. I know I do.

New York
August 1974

How to Hide
Almost Anything

I
Approaches: Pragmatic Object Safety

O, what may man within him hide,
Though angel on the outward side!
                        —SHAKESPEARE

OBJECT SAFETY IS THE OBJECT OF AMERICA. I'M
here to say, "Let me help you." Come home, America, and find
your valuables safe. Or maybe that pouch you like to smoke from
on occasion. Or that special gun you've always had. The one your
father gave you "to protect against snakes." I want to help you
safeguard what you treasure: your bundle of stocks and bonds,
your intimate sex aids, the movie camera you saved six months to
buy, or the old family Bible with its hand-carved stand.

What I offer here is a showroom full of secret compartment
models. You're welcome to browse. Consider it a tour of your own
house. Pick what you want and make it happen. However,
read the entire book before attempting any construction. There
will be no threat of exposure from burglar, police, nor from casual
eyes and fingers. You could hire a carpenter to build it, but you
really should do it yourself. The process of building is surprisingly
refreshing and rejuvenating—it stimulates circulation, and the
accomplishment of finishing such a project is akin to euphoria.
It's so human to build. The actual reason for elation differs psychologically with each builder, of course, like the facades in a
frontier town. But I say, let each person get off on his own secrets—at least let us protect and maintain that last privacy.

Let's take a walk around your apartment or house. Maybe
we can get some ideas of the possibilities here. Oh, this must be

the living room. Charming. Now, what we're looking for are structural items and adornments. The electric outlets and switch-plates, the baseboards running along the walls, leading into the kitchen with the racks and cupboards affixed to the walls, the vents, the pipes, the drains, back into the hall, the coatrack nailed to the wall, the lamps, the bathroom tile, carpeted floors, then into the bedrooms and closets ripe with possibilities. As you scan your eyes over what you're surrounded with, you realize the house that encompasses you is a shell, made up of both hollow and solid members, and complete with all manner of "secondary attachments." You realize those walls, floors, and ceilings offer dead space that can be reached through the "secondary attachments." Once you read this book with that in mind, you'll be ready for another walk through your house, only this time armed with a wealth of specific plans along with your own revitalized ideas.

My sense of fitness of things was injured by the experience I had after building a small secret compartment for a friend. Instead of "hiding" things in *The Closet King* (see page 32) model hidey hole I built into his wall, he used the secret compartment as a novelty, as a curio to show and tell about. He either had untrustworthy friends or the word naturally got around, for when his apartment was burglarized several months later, the compartment was left wide open and the rest of the apartment was untouched. Cash can disappear in wondrous ways.

I want to impress you with this lesson at the very outset. It doesn't matter how selective you are in divulging the existence and whereabouts of the secret place in your home. If it's known by just one other person, your security is breached, as they say in high government circles. Your edge over the dark forces of stealth is compromised, and you'll never be able to rest easy again in the confidence of secrecy. Believe me, it's a contradiction to have a secret place that someone else knows about. Of course the temptation is great. But we mustn't give in.

I guess I'll admit I too am one of those who loves to show off this latest handiwork or well-turned phrase, but in the realm of high domestic subterfuge and concealment, you're asking for trouble if you blow your cover. If you must have a showpiece to brag about, build two secret compartments, completely different in approach and location. Show one; hide your goodies in the other. This is all the warning you'll get. Heed or suffer.

I'd like to say a word for economy. Now I know that, for many, the first inclination will be to pick out a large or difficult plan. But you may be sorry. If you have no need for more than a small, functional hiding place, you risk not finishing if you take on a complicated long-term project. In general, the less carpentry skills you possess, the easier and less complex should be the secret compartment you choose. I've included models for all needs and skills.

For those who rank themselves as neophyte carpenters, there is a section titled "Carpentry" in Special Appendix at the back of the book. Read this, as well as the entire book, and you'll be able to flog your wall with skill and technique.

The body of the book offers specific plans for small, medium, and large-sized secret compartments, even as large as a room, and Special Appendix provides esoteric and tangential information that may prove of use to the more baroque or ambitious secret concealer. For example, in Special Appendix you will find discourse on outdoor, garage, and other miscellaneous secret compartments. You will learn how to hide an affair and how to hide a house. There are also sources and addresses for some items you might want to use.

There is enough information in this book for an ambitious carpenter to start his own business in Iran building secret compartments. Thievery is found the world over. Aside from not having anything worth stealing, the only way to thwart the would-be thief is to put your valuables and secrets out of ready reach. Here are ample approaches and designs, a liberation for whatever secret need: Anyone can have *Object Safety*, one's inalienable human and moral right.

So, come home, America, and find your secrets safe. They can do what they want in Washington or City Hall; they can reshuffle your buying power, ration the food in your belly and the gas in your tank; they can even break into your house, but they can't steal what they can't find. You can protect the secret beating in your breast. As Shakespeare once wrote, "Wherefore are these things hid?"

Don't Miss Special Appendix

2

Some Small Secret Places

Hail, ye small, sweet courtesies of life!
for smooth do ye make the road of it.
                    —Laurence Sterne

THE MOST COMMON, EASIEST TO CONSTRUCT AND
conceal secret apartment is the small one. Because of its limited
size, you can work in and among the *natural* items of your home
without having to adopt more elaborate plans or to reassess and
rearrange your present living environment. The obvious benefit is
that you won't be risking the attention-attracting new element
which could conceivably, either due to size or design, appear out
of phase to a shrewd eye. Good design will, of course, minimize
the possibility of detection. And I should point out that in most
cases you won't have to contend with supersleuths probing your
home, searching each crack and cranny. Thieves look for the fast
and obvious. Their idea of clever concealment is money hidden
under the mattress. Those people who have big things to hide
often do it in bank vaults, in a second set of ledger books, or in
another city where the spouse won't find out. For those who secrete the more mundane yet larger items such as stereo equipment, musical instruments, safes, or even home-grown marijuana
forests, there are appropriately sized designs later in the book.
This chapter and the one that follows are for the modest con-

cealer—the man or woman who has jewelry, a little black book, or a stack of cash, something that one hand can hold without strain.

THE MELLORS MODEL

This secret compartment takes its name from Mellors, the gamekeeper in *Lady Chatterley's Lover,* the novel by D. H. Lawrence. In the early days when I began to name the secret compartments I built, I had to come up with rationalizations for some of the weird names required by the obviously unique nature of my business.

The *Mellors Model* is essentially a pegged coatrack. Since gamekeepers are notorious for having pegged coatracks on their walls, I reasoned, and since Lady Chatterley must have hung her dress somewhere to avoid telltale wrinkles, the *Mellors Model* was clearly the appropriate name for this particular hidey hole.

There are many advantages to this model. It offers easy access at eye level, two features that become better appreciated the longer you use it. Its size is also flexible, so the amount of secret space hidden behind it can vary. The rack may run from three to five feet long and from six to ten inches high. It is an easy model to combine with a security locking device. But the most endearing quality I've found is the ease with which it can be built.

One look at the illustration will unveil most of what you need to construct it. The principle employed here is the one I use on most of my small hiding places: that is, dead space between 2 by 4 wall studs. Unless they are cement, brick, or logs, the walls you are surrounded by have hollow places just waiting to be tapped and used.

Choose the location for your *Mellors Model* wisely. Obviously, should you put it in an unlikely place such as the middle of a living-room wall, it will attract suspicious attention besides raising questions in your friends' minds about your taste. Choose a location where a coatrack would normally be located: in a hallway near the front or back door, or even in a large closet. Be sure to pick an interior wall, not one of the walls that serves as the outer shell of the house. An exterior wall has insulation and other problems connected with it, so it is best to avoid it.

The height of the coatrack should be just above eye level. I can also imagine building a children's *Mellors Model* at a level reachable by those tiny hands of the family. Let's call that the *Baby Mellors Model*. What burglar would suspect that behind those furry parkas and soggy mittens lie Daddy's secret treasures?

The next step is to decide on the board you will use as the back of the coatrack. A simple 1 by 8 pine board three or four feet long will serve admirably. (See below for further variations possible.) Once you've chosen the board, making sure it is not warped and that it is cut to your dimensions with square ends, hold it up to the wall where the compartment and coatrack will be located. Have someone else hold it (if you trust them) while you step back and make sure that is exactly where you want it.

To make it perfectly horizontal, lay a level along the top of the board, adjusting until the bubble reads perfect, then mark the height. Proceed to outline the board with the pencil; draw a line all around the edge right on the wall. Remove the board and you will see graphically the entire area to be hidden by the coatrack. Now, moving in one inch on all sides, make another rectangle inside the first one. (See illustration.) This will give a one-inch support border on all sides, and the inner rectangle will mark the exact opening of the hidey hole, the opening you are now going to make.

The wall you will attack with hammer and chisel will probably be made out of either plaster or plasterboard. If it is made of wood, it is simply a matter of drilling holes at the four corners and using a keyhole saw to cut the rectangle out. But in all likelihood, you'll have to take chisel and hammer in hand and very carefully bang your hole through. One starter method is to drill holes with a brace and bit. To help prevent ragged edges that would require spackle or plaster touchups, run a line of cellophane tape around the outer edges of your inner rectangle. When you're done chiseling your hole, there is no need to remove the tape since it will be hidden behind the coatrack back.

If you are dealing with plaster, after chipping off the external layers, you're going to run up against plaster lathe. These are two-inch strips of quarter-inch wood nailed horizontally to the wall studs from ceiling to floor. I've found the easiest way to break through these is by using an electric drill with a large bit to drill several holes next to one another across the lathe. Cut the rest of the way with a keyhole saw or hammer and chisel. Once

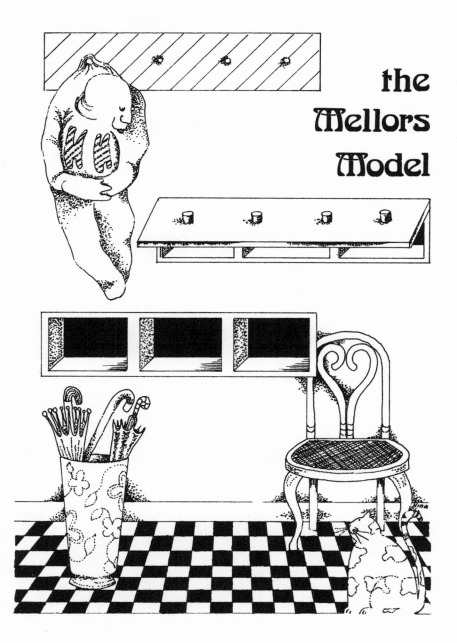

the Mellors Model

you have removed the lathe from the studs, a gaping wall hole, your secret place, is waiting for furnishing.

At this point you will have to decide about the interior of the hidey hole. A slapdash method is to wad stuffing in the bottom of the hole and cover it with spackle. You can also insert a one-inch board as the floor, either flush with the bottom of the hole or sunken an inch or two into the hollow wall. Use epoxy paste, PC-7. I love it. Or you can make little baskets that will hang down in the wall through the hole you've opened. Whatever decision you make, you should tidy up the edges of the hole, using spackling, sandpaper, and paint to smooth out rough edges.

Time to prepare the actual coatrack. There is a great degree of flexibility of design with the *Mellors Model*. As mentioned, you can go with the simple pine board. Like the cheapest casket, this is an honest way to go. No pretentions. Once sanded it can be finished clear, or it can be stained or even painted a nice color to match your decor. A very pleasant effect can be achieved by using a weathered board torn off an old house or abandoned farm outbuilding. Nothing can duplicate the magic in aged wood, the sensual delight in touching it, the distinctive character that only time can bring to it. Just as with people's faces, time reveals truth.

If you happen to be handy with woodcarving or want to pay to have it done, or if you simply want to use good wood, you can buy a hardwood board (mahogany, oak, ash, cherry, maple, etc.) and work it into a beautiful background for the coatrack, a piece of quality to enhance your home and act as a conversation piece when guests enter your door shedding their coats. Be careful that you don't make it too beautiful; otherwise a thief might steal the coatrack itself. From something as simple as beveling the edge of the board all around, you can move to elaborate carving, such as a woodland scene or faces of Presidents you like. What you do with a basic hidey hole design is entirely up to you, and now is the time to start thinking of variations to suit yourself.

Again you have a choice when you come to the coat pegs themselves. Simple one-inch wood dowels cut to the desired length and glued into drilled holes are the simplest approach. You can also use square pegs glued into chiseled-out square holes. You might want to buy ornate metal hooks to adorn the wall.

These can either be purchased new or sought out at distinctive antique shops.

Putting it all together, you have a finished coatrack and a hole to fit it over. All that remains is the means of connecting it to the hidey hole so that you maintain easy access. If you are building now, this is the time to read Chapter 7 on attachments and locking devices: Pick the fastening method that suits your needs. You've come close to that final surge of pleasure, the smile and secure warmth of heart that come from knowing, just as Mellors knew, that you have something no one else has, a special secret.

THE BASIC BASEBOARD

Here is an idea that offers little room for secret storage, but it is one of the easiest and most effective for small items like heirloom jewelry and cash. The first time I looked around my apartment and started thinking of hiding places, this one occurred to me immediately. What runs around your rooms, corner to corner from room to room? The baseboard. It is small, but I've had call to construct several of these for acquaintances who had tobacco-pouch-sized items to hide. Because the baseboard is common to everyone's house or apartment, one rarely takes notice of its presence. When was the last time you looked at your baseboard?

In older houses and apartments, baseboards tend to be large, sometimes as high as one foot, with decorative horizontal lines. Because of this, and also because they are usually covered by countless layers of paint, they are harder to work with; all vestiges of cracks may have been long since covered over. To introduce plausibly integral new cracks is a difficult task indeed. But the higher size of such baseboards does offer more hidden space. If necessary, the difficulties presented here can be gotten around with labor and craftiness.

In newer homes, baseboards are usually made from standard-size hardwood, about four inches high, and they're either stained and finished or painted. Despite the fact that these are easier to work with, the lower height does cramp space behind them. The procedure is basically the same for either a high or low baseboard —to make a section of it removable so that you can utilize the dead space between wall studs. In the case of the modern base-

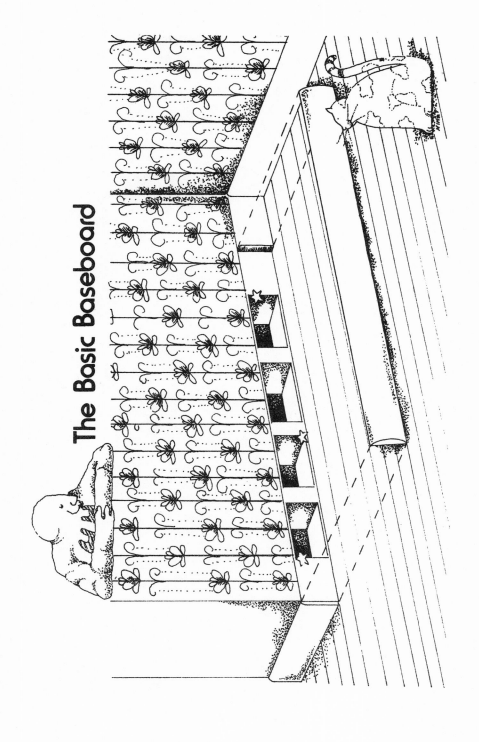

The Basic Baseboard

boards of limited height, one often runs into the problem of the 2 by 4 sill supporting the wall studs. The sill blocks off the usable space and must be dealt with. It only takes work.

This model offers you a choice of any location. Walk around your house examining the baseboards; check closets too. What you are looking for is the method used in fitting them together. If your house was constructed with any care whatsoever, you will have mitered corners. That is, 90-degree junctions in the baseboard will have each board cut at 45-degree angles, fitted together making 90 degrees. Newer ticky-tacky houses sometimes butt one board over the end of the other, making it look terrible to the craftsman, but in this age of functionalism, disposables, and one-bite hamburgers, most people don't care.

As you examine your baseboard, look for a length that can be easily removed. For example, a four- or five-foot piece that comes to the corner of an open doorway or butts against a door jamb. How visible are the cracks where one length of baseboard meets another? Are the cracks filled in and concealed? Too bad. Are they visible? Good. If there are visible cracks, that's all you need. You won't have to worry about prying eyes examining your baseboard for clues as you are now doing. For once you make your removable section of baseboard, even if the crack is a touch more pronounced than the others, it will only appear as if the original carpenter slipped a bit there. Alas—but lucky for you— no one will be offended or even notice.

If you have found a removable section that isn't an un- wieldy length, you're in business. Now, you've got to pry it away from the wall. This either may take a lot of work or the thing could come off in your hand as you tug with fingernails. Most likely, you'll have to use crowbar substitutes like the screw- driver to pry it out. Be careful not to damage the wood or the wall; *work slowly*. But it may be impossible to avoid some dam- age. If so, resign yourself to doing the work necessary to repair it. This can mean painting the entire baseboard when you are done or even painting the whole room. Hopefully, it needed the paint job anyway.

Once the baseboard is pried away from the wall, you'll have to assess the situation. You may meet solid plaster wall right down to the floor, or it may be partially plastered, the workmen being aware that the baseboard would cover it. Another possibility, as mentioned before, is that you may face either wood wall or plasterboard. You know your task—open up the usable space. Use your hammer and chisel or your drill or maybe you like the keyhole saw, whatever, but get to it. Should you run up against a 2 by 4 sill supporting the wall studs, the only thing to do is drill, chip, or chisel out the desired spaces between the wall studs.

For ambitious hidey holers there is always the possibility of completely re-baseboarding a room to give you the kind of innocuous compartment you crave. For example, you might have oversized, high baseboards from the turn of the century. Why should these be any different than an old piece of furniture you salvage from layers of paint? You can strip the paint off the old wood and get down to the grain, making it look like new. And, I might add, it would give you new joining cracks where pieces fit together. These access cracks will be mere shadows in the panorama of woodwork.

There's probably only one fastening device you'll want to consider for this particular hidey hole: the cabinet fastener snap. But I've built some with nail friction fastenings, and Velcro too. Decide for yourself after reading Chapter 7 on fasteners and locks.

Once snapped in place the baseboard secret place is done. You'll sit in a chair with a smug satisfaction. You and no one else will know what that normal-looking wall really contains. Don't look at the baseboard that way too long. Once you've hidden your valuables away, content yourself to visualize the hidey hole in your mind's eye while you get back to the business of questing a pleasant life rhythm.

THE CLOSET KING

Closets are a way of life to many. For some people, the joy of opening a closet and basking in the task of choosing evening wear is like standing naked face front to a newly risen hot summer sun, remote lake waters tickling the toes. Some children spend so much time in closets, one might think them toy-box sleepers. You know, those creepy kids who sleep in poor boxes, the wood lids covering them with a Transylvanian shadow. I'm one of those people who uses a closet as a dump for all things to be sorted, cleaned, stored, temporarily hidden, or suppressed, repressed, left unbidden.

the Closet King

Did you ever pay attention to the board that runs along the sidewalls of a closet, just under the clothes-hanging pole? Of course, some closets don't have them, but they are very common, serving as functional support. You can add them to an apartment and no one will notice. It's like putting another stripe on a sergeant. What a perfect location for a hidey hole. It's at a convenient height. If your clothes aren't too crowded in the closet, the access is easy. And special craftsmanship isn't required. These boards vary from a couple of inches to half a foot in height, and the length of hidden space between studs is up to you. If you like, you can even put a compartment behind both of the support boards on either side of the closet.

The first step is to remove the board, prying *carefully* from the wall to avoid plaster disaster. You're likely to meet variations of construction, but the main job is to get that board off the wall with a minimum of damage. Once done, make sure the hanger pole is independently stable enough for the weight of hanging clothes. The remainder of the task is almost identical to the *Mellors Model*; finish the interior of the hole, then choose the mounting and access method from Chapter 7.

You might want to repaint when you're finished building the *Closet King*. One coat won't take much work or paint, and it will ensure that the whole closet is uniform in color and mood, leaving the unsuspecting still unsuspecting. It wouldn't be wise to strip paint from these boards or otherwise draw attention to them.

There are, of course, many ways to finish the inside of a hidey hole once you've opened the space. Usually I perform the most easy and functional by simply painting it a bright attractive color.

THE DOOR JAMB SAFE

One of the prettiest hidey holes going, I'd say. What could be more integral to an apartment or house than the doorway, the portal to another place, from space to space. People stand in doorways, teen-agers drink Cokes there, children hang and swing, light comes through the opening, and that's also where a door shuts with authority. What better or handier place for a hidey hole than the spacy dimension changer where people pass without giving second thoughts. The door.

But: the more you want it the more you've got to take. Or,

take it. And so, to complete this charming secret compartment, you must do more extensive work. You may even have to rebuild your doorframe. If you're fit for such a challenge, take a proper crowbar in your strong hands. Get to work and use a little of that lever theory. If not careful, however, you could end up ripping the wood apart while yanking it from its nails. Well, that's all right, it releases aggressions. You can be a better woman or man because of it, cleansed. You can always buy a new set of door jamb boards from your lumberyard. Unless, that is, you are working with a fancy one-of-a-kind door jamb and molding treatment. If you have that kind of woodwork, don't undertake a hidey hole like this unless you are a very good carpenter.

Door jambs are usually an upside-down "U" of 1 by 6s or 1 by 8s nailed into place. On the face of the board there may be narrow strips of wooden molding—called *stop* molding—tacked on. And around the outside edge of the door, covering the crack between board and wall, is a wide molding. Usually this is simple and unadorned, joined at the corners with mitered angles.

The job is to remove the side door jamb board, the one opposite where the door is hinged. You may have to remove the entire door jamb to accomplish this successfully. It is vital, as a first step, to remove the small stop molding across the top of the doorframe. This permits you to pry the doorframe side from the wall. Hang onto this stop molding until the absolute end.

With the door jamb side removed, we have to guarantee the support of the top crossing board. If it isn't already nailed in place, do so now. Carefully pound in the nails without marring the surfaces with unneeded wood dents.

What you're left with is a side to the door jamb, loose in your hands, the end of the wall over which it fits, and the assorted moldings you may have removed in freeing the side-board. The easiest hinge/fulcrum arrangement for this hidey hole is to use the protruding-nails-from-the-end-of-the-board technique. See the illustration. The nails at the bottom edge of the board should fit into corresponding holes in the floor at the base of the doorframe. After making the holes, you will have to work them open a bit with the nail and hammer so that the board will pull open freely at the top without binding or bending nails at the fulcrum base.

the Door Jamb Safe

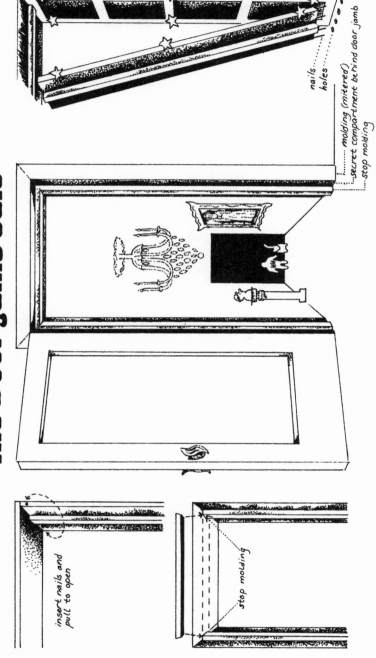

insert nails and pull to open

stop molding

molding (mitered)
secret compartment behind door jamb
stop molding

nails
holes

Nina

Now you can set the board against the base of the doorway, the nails in the holes, and swing it up against the wall into place. To avoid undue binding against the top plate, you can bevel off the rubbing edge with a rasp and sandpaper. The edge will be covered up by molding, invisible when the construct is completed. If the jamb moves in and out of place perfectly, then you can take it out of its holes and set it aside for a while. You have to hollow out your secret compartment now.

You are confronted with the end edge of the wall. It most likely will be the end wall stud embellished with plaster. Whatever you meet, you'll have to ad lib. The idea is to make space for valuables. You probably won't be able to make big compartments. For example, if you meet the end wall stud, it wouldn't be wise to weaken the structure of the wall by cutting it completely through at this point. You may find it practical to make only a number of very small cubbyholes down the length of the exposed wall. This would be suitable, of course, for jewelry, money, or aphrodisiacs. If you want to make larger spaces here, it will take a major operation on the wall itself—tearing down and replastering.

After completing the interior of the hidey hole, set the jamb section back in place and read Chapter 7 to decide which connecting or locking device you will use. It'll probably be cabinet fastener snaps. Whatever you use, install these at the top and middle of the board and test it several times, making sure it opens and closes, snapping the door jamb into place. The easiest way to pull it open is to pound a small nail hole in the upper corners: Insert a nail or pick into each hole, pull toward yourself, and the board will swing open. Notice the location of the innocent-looking holes in the illustration.

Close the hidey hole. Now carefully align and replace the molding around the doorframe, using the original nail holes. This will cover the edge crack of the board over your hidey hole. Try to nail the molding lightly against the jamb. Once in place, you have to open and close your secret door, sanding the points that rub until you have mobility without excessive friction. Efficiency.

There is only one piece of work remaining in the construction stage. That is to replace the stop molding on the top of the doorframe. If you sand very carefully, you might get by sliding it into a snug fit. Angles of a miter-cut end would hold it in place. But you'll probably want to use magnets and plates to lock it in with more authority. This is an important and crucial phase of your operation and you must not, indeed will not, settle for less than perfection. The stop molding has to be removed each time you open the secret compartment, yet it must look solid and normal when in place. Once this is prepared for final installation, you can repair any visual damage you've caused the doorframe.

When painting the door jamb, don't flood the joining cracks runny. Spare the area excessive paint so that the cracks around the top stop molding won't stand out. After painting or refinishing your door jamb, you'll have to make some minor adjustments until the removable piece of stop molding slides in and out of place with ease; then, a hearty tug and the door side opens, revealing your more than six feet of secrecy.

Done, breathe deeply, from the stomach, step back, and take a look at your handiwork. Nothing visible calls attention to the secret the door jamb holds. You've done it! And you'll never regret it.

THE SPICE NOOK

There are all kinds of spice rack arrangements. Handy people make their own. It can be a closed-in cabinet or just a long shelf on which a gamut of spices are readily accessible for creative cooking. Ordinarily, I'm in sympathy with doing things creatively instead of by rote or from mediocre example. Still, in the case of this particular hidey hole, you can easily use one of those commercially designed and constructed spice racks available in fine stores everywhere. If you're one of those Americans who limits himself to salt and pepper and shuns the basil, oregano, and curry, it won't hurt you to buy a ready-to-use spice rack and actually try the spices in different dishes. But before I succumb to the urge to include recipes, let's look at the kind of spice rack you'll need for constructing this secret little kitchen nook.

Cheaply designed spice racks come in various sizes and shapes. There is but one requirement: There must be a back to it to use as the door to your secret compartment in the wall. Some types will permit you to add a hardboard or quarter-inch plywood back to them. This is all perfectly suitable. But the most

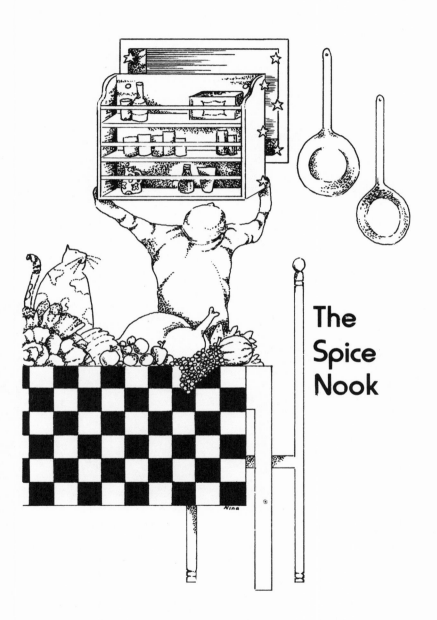

The
Spice
Nook

satisfying *Spice Nook,* from my point of view, is a rack made from scratch.

Take some time off from frenetic concerns. Relax, get out some tools, and design a spice rack, the size, design, line, and even feel of which will be yours. A small mark in a plastic world, true, yet one that counts nonetheless, saying, "There is still practical craftsmanship. There are still people who make the things around them with caring hands."

One reason I think care and concern should be taken with the spice rack itself is that it's about the only thing you have to do in constructing this hidey hole. Pounding a hole in the wall, aaa, that's nothing. You should see the spice rack my cousin's wife made.

Once you have a completed spice rack with a back, either square or rectangular, stained dark, light, or painted, hold it up to the wall where you plan to hang it. Just like the *Mellors Model* you have to trace the shape of it with a pencil on the wall. Put the rack aside. Although it is discussed more fully in Chapter 7, I think this is a good point to recommend the false bolt technique, or even the false nail technique. There is something mighty satisfying and convincing about seeing a spice rack "attached" to the wall with four shiny bolt heads and circular washers. In reality, of course, they're a ruse to fool snoopy intruders into believing that the spice rack is firmly bolt-screwed into the wall. (See Chapter 7.)

Now the wall is staring at you with the pencil outline of the spice rack drawn on it. If you remember the seminal *Mellors Model,* you know what happens next. Carve a hidey hole into that solid wall. Take drill, hammer, chisel, keyhole saw in hand. Dance in front of the wall shaking your tools, eyeing the spot. This is called the meditative pre-step. As in baseball, serenity is a sure winner. Don't hesitate when the voice in your ear speaks. Do.

You must remember to leave an inch or so support border of wall around the edges of the actual hole to fit snugly against the back of the rack. I've found colorful contact paper satisfying as an interior decoration for a kitchen hiding place such as this. Like a crisp salad of watercress, Chapter 7 awaits you and your choice of fastening for final installation.

ELEMENTARY SECRET PANEL

There must exist somewhere a quiet unassuming craftsman who has the knowledge and skills to make masterwork secret panels. I believe this because I've seen countless movies and books in which mysterious and fictional secret panels appeared to satisfy my romantic imagination. I believe this with all my heart and soul. Unfortunately, it isn't me. I don't possess the knowledge and skill to make the kind of electric sliding panels one sees juxtaposed to Hollywood swimming pools late at night in the tube light. I do have a more ethnic version, however: See Special Appendix, *Slick Sliding Panel*. Here, I postulate a plan for a rather complicated little number, yet one that's pristine in its elemental functionalism.

In reality, I've seen only one secret panel by another's hands. It was very elementary. Essentially, a secret panel, as I define it, is a movable unit of wood integral to some larger and camouflaging construct. We all know the classic example of a luxurious office or den with walls paneled in designs of ornate wood. A square or rectangular section, looking like many other panels in the wall, has the potential to be opened by the person with knowledge. Most of us don't live in that kind of world but there are cheaper variations of the same idea that we can use.

All you need is some kind of wood construct on your walls. Many people have rumpus rooms or porches paneled in knotty pine boards. Unfortunately, the paneling that goes up in most homes today is that ugly pre-finished four-foot-by-eight-foot quarter-inch plywood from the Philippines. Not only is it a further encroachment of masticated architecture, but it isn't easily adaptable to secret-compartment construction. Those fake cracks that run up and down the plywood, trying to look like boards joining, are so unreal that if you tried to cut and piece together a secret panel, making a real crack along one of those lines, it would be visibly obvious to even a casual glance.

I have seen a few examples of very beautiful wood paneling, however. It shows that it is still possible to take a little care in the atmosphere we surround ourselves with. And it really isn't very difficult or complicated to nail wood boards to a wall to make an attractive paneled wall. Hammer, nails, and a little bit of money for wood, that's all it takes. I've seen walls wonderfully

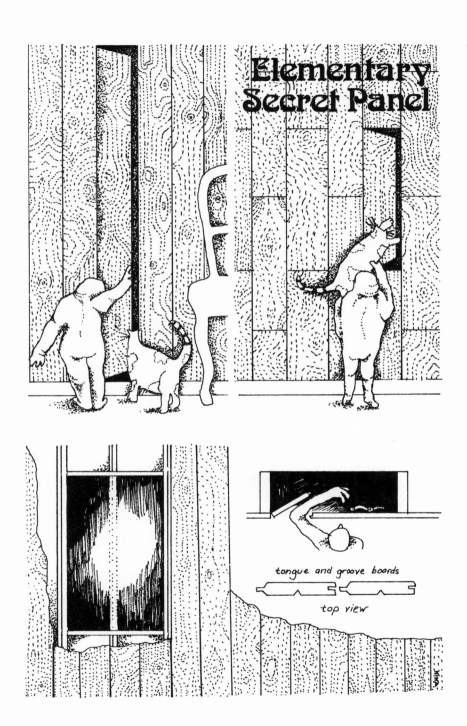

Elementary Secret Panel

tongue and groove boards

top view

paneled with weathered and bleached boards taken from old farm buildings. So, for the person who has everything including energy and desire, but who lacks a paneled wall, it's only a few hours of labor away. And, naturally, while you're about it, you might as well include a secret panel.

The secret space will again fall between wall studs. Let your eyes rove around the house until the proper location comes to you. You could panel one wall of the living room, or the entry way near the front door, or a wall of the master bedroom or dining room. Once that's decided, you'll have to consider the decor in that area of the house and judge what kind of wood paneling you want. There are light and dark woods that can be finished either clear or stained to the color you wish. Of course, I would try to dissuade anyone who wanted to paint good wood. I can, however, imagine certain people with weird tendencies, possessed of little money, who could make this compartment out of cheap pine, painting the boards in different colors creating stripes. Red and white is a nice traditional. Any straight hardwood makes excellent paneling. I like to use beveled tongue-and-groove pine boards between six and ten inches in width. Plain, square-edged boards can be used as well, but the joining cracks must be dealt with much more carefully.

The idea is to nail the paneling in place on the wall, making one of the boards movable. You'll be able to push the board inward and reach the secret compartment. There are two possible approaches. You can make a floor-to-ceiling access panel. See the illustration. Or, for a smaller door opening, you can vary the lengths of boards nailed to the wall, making horizontal cracks appear at odd intervals. I prefer the latter—it's more attractive.

Before beginning to nail up the paneling, choose the area of the wall that will be the hidey hole. Once again, it is simply a matter of hammer and chisel, drill and saw dirty work. Open up a hole between two walls studs. This will give you a compartment as wide as sixteen inches—depending on the distance between wall studs—with whatever height you choose to hollow out. Now move to the side of the hole and open it up wider, reaching across the wall stud, clearing a hole of the same height over to the next wall stud. That leaves one vertical stud exposed in the middle of your secret place. The illustration shows how that center stud has to be cut and removed. Cut it across the top and the bottom of the hole and pry the piece out to convert the two compartments into one. This done, use 2 by 4s to nail crosspieces at the top and bottom for support. I've chosen to illustrate a secret compartment of a handy three-foot size. This means, of course, that the board that serves as your panel door can be only three feet in height in order to open inward into the wall. There is a top view provided. You can see that the panel can open only a limited amount. This is due to the width of the board and the amount of depth provided between wall studs; the panel swings in only far enough to permit your arm access. You reach in and to the right into the open space behind the wall paneling. Most likely, you'll want to build several shelves in the compartment to accommodate more items. If so, the time to do that is now, before putting the paneling up.

If you plan on using square-edged boards for paneling, wood without grooved or beveled edges, I'd recommend first painting the wall area with black paint. This will permit slight cracks between boards, making all the cracks uniformly dark. As a result, the cracks around the secret panel will look no different.

Once the inside of the secret compartment is finished to your satisfaction, the task of nailing the wall paneling comes next. Start at one end and make a vertical line on the wall, a line that is perfectly straight up and down. An easy way to achieve this is to use a plumb bob, or simply a string with a weight hanging from it. Hang this down the wall where the paneling will begin, draw your pencil line, and you'll have a perfect vertical to begin your first board. If you want to spend a bit more money, a chalk line expedites this process and is especially handy when you have a long wall to panel, requiring several vertical lines as you progress for perfect alignment. Although it is unlikely you'd go astray enough to notice visually, the alignments must be perfect at the entrance point to the hidey hole. Otherwise, you may have trouble installing a panel that will be both innocuous and perfect in function.

It doesn't matter at which end of the wall you begin, but once you reach the location of the opening panel, suspend all work on the paneling to install the secret panel itself. The actual method of attachment will probably be spring hinges and magnetic fasteners. But to decide on this aspect of the compartment construction, turn to popular Chapter 7.

You can employ many variations of this basic approach. The chief principle is a construct on the wall with one integral part that opens inward to reveal hidden space. Thus you can make elaborate wall panels of your own design. One good idea is to panel only halfway up the wall culminating at a chest-high shelf. Tudor board decor can offer a multitude of possibilities and is discussed later. An extremely ambitious variation of the approach can be found in Chapter 4, *Inset Wall Space.*

All of the compartments discussed in this chapter have employed the dead space between wall studs. The following chapter offers other approaches to the small secret place. For those who want to use one of the plans just discussed yet would prefer a greater depth to the compartment, one technique is explained in Special Appendix under the listing, *Wall Expansion.*

By now you must be getting a feel for secret compartment construction. Already, your mind is spinning off its own ideas. Keep reading with that creative curiosity, for there are all manner of bizarre ideas to come.

Only 88 Pages to Special Appendix

3
More Small Ones but Good Ones

. . . the world is small when your enemy is loose on the other side.
—JOHN BOYLE O'REILLY

AMERICA IS LIKE A STRAWBERRY PATCH. THE FIRST cycle is a barren one as it was with our motherland's early decades of struggle to survive. Then comes the ripe fruit of reproduction followed gently by animal thieves. From a Puritan heritage as harsh as the rocky shore that first harbored it, our plenitude has grown by the hands of labor and the devices of exploitation. I exploit, you exploit, he or she exploits. Now we stick our fingers in a pie that grows cold. The frontiers have become one, ourselves. As a small by-product, we are beginning to realize that big is not always best. Once we were grateful for each fish caught, a food supply. But who wants to catch a small fish now? Who wants to be a small fish, cash a small check, save pennies, be short, eat beans, or drive a small car that is black? Those people who find themselves with little choice, that's who. And like nostalgia, a cobwebless past, more of us each day find that reverting is not only sentimentally pleasing but psychologically practical, even necessary.

To try to get a grasp on this morass, real Americans must place hidey-hole construction in a greater context. It can be size. How big is yours? What ever happened to Tiny Tim? Who is shorter than his or her parents? How many artists still paint miniatures or play miniature golf? Are we to understand that the attrition rate of *small* is an evolutionary good? Are values blandly handed to us to be blindly accepted? I think not.

Harlan was the smallest American I've ever met. He was pygmy-sized, ostracized, economized, a genuine old-fashioned immigrant who had never savored America's sweeter juices. He lived in a fifth floor walk-up in the Yorktown area of Manhattan. Besides being small, he was old. It seems that there are two strikes against him already. I should have been quicker to pick up on the weird vibrations when I heard his voice on the phone, a little voice, "I vant hidey hole."

I knocked on his door. The spyhole was mounted at the height of my sternum. I heard him on the other side of the door, peeking at me, seeing nothing but my blue work shirt.

"Vat is it you vant? Go vay."

I introduced myself.

"How do I know it is you?"

I bent down so he could see me. I smiled. "You asked for my card on the street. Remember my face?"

"It is you, all right." He unlocked the door, and I saw that he was a tiny man, yet short of being a proper midget, with gray hair, gray stubble on his chin, and beady eyes. Blue baggy pants were held up by suspenders, and he wore a dirt-soiled vest over his shirt. He looked like an etching. His wet eyes were on me constantly as we went through the preliminaries.

"I don't have money," he said. "How much you charge?"

I reminded him of my sales brochure and the $100 base price.

"I don't have money."

I was beginning to get the idea. I said, "You want I should go?"

"I don't vant you should go. I am old man. I don't have money. How much to make a small hidey hole for me?"

I asked how big he wanted it. How often he had to get at it and he kept saying things like, "A small one. I don't need big. I don't have money."

The apartment was two rooms. The landlord had never painted it. It had mummy-colored wallpaper from an obscure decade. Working under such circumstances, any new construct would be as difficult to disguise as a hard hat full of caviar.

I finally cornered him into saying he needed a space big

enough for a coin purse. "I don't have much to hide," said the glint-eyed old man. I wanted out of the situation fast, so I suggested the economical and easy electric outlet approach. He seized my meaning immediately.

"You can do that? You come back tomorrow night, same time. I have electric plates for you. We talk about price. Thank you, thank you." He reached up to shake my hand with great gratitude and eased me out the door.

I kept wondering about the plural he used, "plates." And sure enough the next evening he had more than one electric plug outlet. He had five of them.

"You see? I got for you." His smile was electric; he seemed so proud. "Now you can fix. Three in this room and two in that, please."

I first argued. "Mr. Harlan. It's too obvious to have so many new plug outlets in an old flophouse like this." But Harlan's smile did not lose momentum. He was clearly in charge of the situation, so now nothing could stand in his way. Certainly not me.

"Mr. Secret Compartment man," he said, languoring the words on his slack lips, "you put two behind the sofa and one over there behind the vanity, God bless her soul. You fix three here, two in there. Nobody look twice. They stupid. You fix it and I am happy."

So I fixed them, considered myself lucky, even honored to accept one hundred dollars for all my labors and left his apartment building whistling into a very nice evening.

The electric outlet hidey hole is probably the easiest and quickest to construct. You simply make use of space behind a false electrical outlet. This includes light switches, blank plates, and those plug-in places. Such a compartment is a bit facile for my taste, somewhat more prone to discovery (police look there), and very limited in size. But you can't argue with the benefits of speed and efficiency of construction and the ready accessibility it permits.

ELECTRIC PLUG AND OUTLET SUBTERFUGE

The first step in construction is the choice: either build a new hole to be covered by the plug plate or, conversely, convert an already existing outlet to neuter status. The conversion is a rather simple affair, so I'll discuss that first.

Choose your plate. Cut the electricity. This can be done by opening the master switch or unscrewing the applicable fuse. Whatever you do, make absolutely sure the electricity is off before touching the innards of an electrical system.

Using a screwdriver, it is a simple matter to remove the plastic plate over the outlet itself. Once inside, the task is to disconnect the electrical wires from the switch or plug. You may unscrew the leads or cut the wires with a heavy wirecutter. Once done, the ends of the two *hot* lines should be wrapped in electricians' tape to nullify them. Either push them back out of the way or remove the entire outlet box for a bit more space; then bend the wires out of the way.

If you are using an electric plug-in plate, remove the plug faces from their terminal and glue them in place in the appropriate holes of the plate. A similar process is necessary for light switches. You have to remove the switch knob itself and anchor it to the switch plate with glue or any other means.

The real job is choosing the method of attachment. It's important. If you are satisfied with a tiny space, you can leave the box intact and use the original screws to remove or close the plate. But if you enlarge the hole by removing the metal electric box, you will be removing the purchase for the plate screw. In such a case, you may want to use the simple tape, or Velcro techniques described in Chapter 7. If so, cut off the screw and glue the head in place on the plate.

Though it may be low quality security, it is great for stuffing love letters, gold coins, and well-intentioned messages to yourself. It fits on most any wall becoming as obscure as integration. When that salesman at the door really does have something you want, or when the burglar needs a little something so he'll leave happy, the *Electric Outlet* is a handy hidey hole for ready cash. I really think, though, it will only whet your appetite for something better. And so we'll now move on.

THE BOOK BASEMENT
This is a down-to-earth hidey hole, yet one with a lot of class. It adapts well to both roughshod and craftsmanlike methods. You can build one in a bookcase you already own, either antique or modern, or you can build one from scratch. There is one cautionary note for those who tackle an already assembled bookcase.

You may have to strip and refinish the entire piece to hide the effects of your carpentry.

Most bookcases have their lower shelf raised at least a few inches from the floor with a crossing baseboard in the front, hiding the dead space. That "hole" under the lower shelf can be of considerable size. Certainly enough room for handfuls of goodies.

All we have to do to use that secret space is to make the bottom shelf removable. The simplest approach would have you merely resting the snug-fitting bottom shelf in place and placing a few books or other items on it. All that would be required to reach the space would be to move the objects and lift the shelf. We can elaborate on that basic plan by using a hinge device to anchor one side and make the other end snap into place with a fastening device. This would be similar to closing the top of an ammunition canister, or the center console compartment in a Mustang.

It is easy to appreciate the aesthetic simplicity of this design; gravity holds it together and as part of a functioning bookcase, nothing could be more innocuously functional. Important people like lawyers have asked me to build this model.

If you are constructing the bookcase, simply cut and nail all shelves save the bottom one. This last should be cut to fit perfectly with a slight crack for leeway in lifting. It might be necessary to sand the ends of the board to permit the shelf to swing up without undue friction. Once the shelf fits in place, you will probably want to employ fasteners. For methodology refer to the last chapter. This design lends itself well to the nail secret-locking device.

THE WOOD PILE

If you are willing to step down into the funky arena, try the *Wood Pile*. Here is a way to boldly flaunt your hidey hole all the while smiling into the teeth of guests. Put a hidey hole in your woodbin. I've had a hidey hole in my wood pile, and it was a downright secure feeling. To know, in the fear of the moment, that a secret hole nestles in one of those logs, waiting to do duty. It's a portable servant. Take your log with you wherever you go. It isn't out of place at the beach, camping, or in the occasional mobile home. Just remember to camouflage it well and don't get caught carrying it alone.

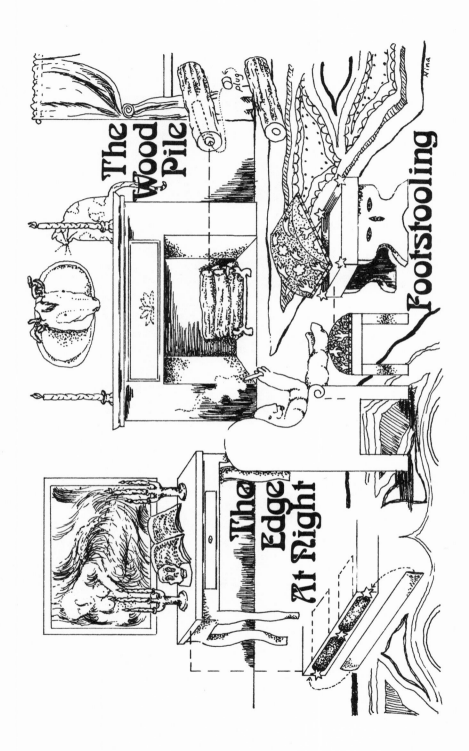

To make it, you need a couple of average-looking square-end cut fireplace-style logs. You will hollow out a compartment in an end of one log. Using an electric drill with as large a bit as possible, drill and chisel open a round compartment two to four inches wide and five to ten inches deep. You might want to use the drill with a round-head rasp to shape the opening of the hole.

Once the hole is prepared, you have to cut a circle from the other log that will realistically plug the hole. Cut a one-and-a-half-inch deep slice off the end of the second log. Make a pattern with paper and draw the size and shape of the plug you need right on the slab of log. To cut the plug out, use a coping or saber saw. Or you can make four cuts with a handsaw and then use the electric drill and rasp to shave off the corners. Do the final shaping very carefully. You want to make the round plug as perfect a fit for the hole as possible. Once the plug is in place and flush with the face of the log, you may have trouble removing it. Take two knives, insert in the cracks on opposite sides of the plug and lift out. Another entrance device for this compartment is the magnet pull explained in Chapter 7.

Obviously you won't be able to make the crack around the plug disappear. But it will be concentric with the age circles in the wood and that can't be bad. Still and yet, close scrutiny could undo you. So admittedly, this is a high risk approach to SeComp design. But it's solid, if you can brazen it out. What do you have to worry about? You think people look at your logs? Just don't burn it.

THE EDGE AT NIGHT

When the burglars creep in a window, you won't have to say you're sorry if you have an *Edge at Night* hidey hole. This model comes right down there around your hands, easy to stick your fingers into, a hole in the edge of your desk or table.

Many tables and desks have decorative moldings around the edges of their circumference. They can also be added to tables with squared edges. Here's how you do it.

Choose an edge of the desk or table that will be less frequently used and proceed to draw with pencil an outline of the area you want to hollow out. You know from discourse on previous hidey holes that the best approach is the aggressive one. God knows we need a sane and healthy outlet for the overwhelming aggressions we foster. So here's your way to avoid becoming a homicidal maniac; aggressively attack that little penciled space. Take your electric drill or brace and bit and attack! You may also do yeoman chiseling and erode the space. Drill and chisel and sweat and beat; get that hidey hole space you need. Smooth it out so you like to touch it. Rasp, sandpaper, and oil the grain.

Now, assuming you have cut molding to put around the edge of the desk, proceed to nail the three normal sides in place. Glue is also permitted. If you've measured and cut well, the last piece of molding should fit perfectly into place, over the edge of the desk, covering your hallowed hole. Make whatever adjustments are necessary to assure a perfect fit so no notice will be drawn to it.

There remains the fastening technique. Chapter 7 will show that the friction nail, magnet fastener, and Velcro methods work well in the *Edge at Night*.

This hidey hole is close to my heart since I work at a desk now. To have that little hidden space only an arm's length away salves my anxieties. Reach out there and touch the smooth sides of that secret place and confidence comes to you. You gain an edge. You will win more days and lose less nights in the little world league of life players.

FOOTSTOOLING

Footstooling is a rare craft thought to have originated in Croatia for wealthy patrons, the classic archetypes of the form being designed by Fernando Fernando II. Since, however, this theory as well as all others are suspect, turn your attention to the form and not the formulators. What do we have here? A footstool. Or the idea "footstool," covering diverse representations. The first reaction is, "good location." And that's correct. A good location for a secret compartment of a lesser class security. It can be a charmer, a real smoothy.

My footstooling experience is limited, alas, so I can't give you the locations of the eight or ten classic Fernandos. But I think an excellent introduction to the genre of footstooling will be had by building a rather grand yet simple footstool, named simply that. It is reputed to be a bastard Shaker creation, a foggy mind going solo one sinful day back then.

You will want to use two-inch hardwood boards. Boards that

are twelve or fourteen inches wide, well seasoned, and not warped. These will form the ends or legs of the stool. See the illustration. Some hardwood boards of lesser size will also be required, according to your design. The basic object is a simple stool with cutouts for harmonious design. You shape the two endboards into whatever configuration you desire, using drill, saws, and even woodworking chisels. Cutouts in the middle of the board can be especially dramatic. For example, a teardrop hole cut out of the wood with a coping saw, or a four-leaf clover, a bell, slices of moon, a simulated rifle scope. Once again you are called upon to use your artistic sense.

The two long boards on the sides are, of course, the legs that support the top where four- or six-inch boards cross and form a rectangular box. You should join these pieces with very solid joints, whether you make elaborate joint cuttings or use angle irons and glue. Mitered cuts at the corners aid the flow of line.

You must put a floor in that compartment that's forming at the top of the footstool. This can be made from hardwood or plywood and will fit snugly on all sides.

Set up on its legs, the footstool now has a compartment in the top, three or five inches deep. You look down into a lovely, large square or rectangle which you will presently hide with the cushioned top of the footrest.

The board that will close over the hole in the footstool, the door, as it were, should be made from a wide hardwood board. It should have at least a small overhang all around when in place so that the actual junction crack is not noticed. Upon this board door, you must now construct a cushion. I have a preference for the lumpy hillocks of foam, shaped something like grandma's pies. But you can also use flat foam tops enclosed in fabric and tacked tautly in place on the board. I don't think the Shakers would approve of foam rubber but you can shape it with a razor, or you can sandwich a lower strip of foam with an upper pillow of feathers.

Fastening the top to the base of the footstool, you will find, is similar to the technique of the *Mellors Model*. Chapter 7, once again, will help you.

If you've taken pride and care, you have created a beautiful piece of furniture. You will overhear friends saying, "robust wood," "attractively functional." Isn't that what makes all the effort worthwhile? You will have to choose a stain or finish for your creation. Make sure it is sanded smooth. On cold, lonely nights when the wind runs up the chimney, you may find yourself more than once caressing the curves of your design. There is a saying in Croatia that applies: "A footstool can soothe the nerves, if you pay it."

GOING DOWN A DRAIN

Going Down a Drain is simple if you have a basement drain, one set in the cement floor, with a wide drainage pipe sinking out of sight. With no drain to fit the bill, don't despair, you other basement owners. You can create one.

First let me talk with you lucky ones who have floor drains. Take a screwdriver or other tool, if your drain is peculiar, and remove the drain grill covering the flush hole. Look inside. Is it a wide pipe falling away into darkness? Good. All you have to do is hang a waterproof bag securely so it doesn't wash away should your basement get wet. Properly secured, with room for the drain to function normally, your hidey hole is ready for the door, the lid, in this case the metal grill with the rusted drain holes. Screw it back in place over the hole and you have frustrated the great rank and file of burglars.

In constructing *Going Down a Drain* from scratch, you can ignore the possibility of flooding and hope it never happens. This would entail excavating a hole in your cement floor that goes nowhere, the first place to fill with water should a gush develop. Plastic bags are handy in such cases. If this arrangement will protect what you're hiding, proceed as follows. Choose a piece of floor that is not obviously high ground. Plausible drains are always located at the lowest spot of a slanting floor. But if the incline is not too great, you can get away with installing a false drain in a convenient out-of-the-way place, maybe even under the edge of a workbench or that couch the animals ravished.

You are going to have to pickax, hammer, and punch a hole into your cement floor. You may run into drainage pipes, if you're not careful, or metal reinforcing rods. Nobody said this was going to be easy. Once you have a foot-deep compartment, you can sink a large four- or six-inch pipe into the space and cement it up. Arrange for the top to accept the screw-on grill plate. The

Franciscan Footlocker

Humped Pipes →

Going Down A Drain

Tape

A and B

threaded cap

Franciscan Footlocker

threaded pipe

cement work around the top of the drain must be very efficient looking, slanting toward the drain smoothly.

Once the cement is dry, check out how it looks. Stands out like a maniac supervisor, doesn't it? Take some oil, common dirt, or yellowing polish, and rub it in there. Make that whole area of the floor look ugly if you have to, like a dirty old drain, if you have to. Don't be ashamed of it. The dirtier it looks, the more natural you look.

HUMPED PIPES

Humped Pipes is, of course, a lower class idiomatic expression for necked pipe sections. You see versions of the same linear principle all around you: those huge snouted vent pipes on ships, a shepherd's staff, a hung suspect, drooped flowers, or a delicate young girl looking into an isolated pool at her toes.

Now that you stop to think about it, you realize you've seen pipes arching up and over like this before, in sidewalks, basements—very common in shoddy basement apartments. Others of you may have noticed a peculiar thing. Such pipes sometimes occur in large buildings as a plumber's whimsy or an architectural snafu. In any event, nothing repulses glances better than grungy pipes. If you don't have a basement situation to employ *Humped Pipes,* you could get away with putting one under your sink. Yes, that place that doesn't really do anything well. Take up a corner of that space and install a *Humped Pipe.*

In cement floors you will merely chisel out enough of a hole to cement the pipe in place, giving it that tied-to-greater-things-down-below look. If you are working at the bottom of a kitchen-sink cabinet, you may have to cut a hole for the pipe through tin, wood, or some other substance. Obviously, you have to make that pipe coming up through a hole in the bottom of the cabinet look natural, as though it were installed ten years ago. If you have a new pipe, chip it, scratch it, besmirch it. Nest a spider in the upper regions and you might as well cement around the base hole. Make it look anchored, a mysterious apparition of metal under the sink. A touch filthy. Who would want to stick his hand up in there. You will.

A simple method to use for getting the booty out of this hidey hole is a money bag with a thong tied around the top. Throw your bundle into the pipe and hang onto the long thong.

A square of duct tape will hold this string in place so you can reach up into the neck of the pipe, find the string, and then remove your hideables.

THE FRANCISCAN FOOTLOCKER

If you have a secret compulsion to hide a hole beneath your floor, consider squares. Floor tile and parquet flooring offer square sections in great abundance. We can pick the lucky square, remove it, and put a hidey hole under it. If there is cement under floor tile, I wouldn't recommend it. But for most common folks this approach has possibilities. Everybody knows about movable boards as egress into the dead floor space. But one of many squares, that has class. As in end-play strategy or jungle stalking, your camouflage will be as secure as your skill. Who is going to go around examining your parquet floor parts?

As always, you have to do a real smooth job, aligning the tile or wood squares carefully. One corner sticking up would break the pattern and draw attention. You may have to retile your floor to get the right effect, but you can pick a small room for the installation. If you can remove one square without undue damage to the edges, hooray! Some asbestos tiles can be heated with a portable torch so that the adhesive under them loosens. I wouldn't get into this unless you know what you're dealing with and what you're doing. On the other hand, anyone can lay floor tile. It's like playing with blocks.

Once you have prepared the entrance square, cut a hole in the floor with a keyhole or saber saw, or if problems arise, deal with the floor space presented you. There may be simple empty space as much as a foot deep. Or you might have to work in and around beams or other structural members. One handy enclosure method is to use pipe, a four-, six-, or eight-inch pipe, threaded at the top to accept a screw-in plate. You see this sort of plumbing and lid arrangement imbedded in sidewalks and floor basements. With the solemn-looking metal plug circled into place, an intruder's first thoughts would be, "Water main, gas leak, telephone explosion, taboo, no no." It is a stunning second front against the sneers and intent of the alien creeper. Sink one of these babies under a floor tile or parquet block and you'll be cooking with conspiracy.

Now, you're ready to select the fastening method for the

top, the tile, your door. I've always had a genuine fondness for Velcro. Magnets and duct tape approach work. You could even suck up the secret square with a toilet plunger.

If your hands can be gentle enough, deft enough, you can make a wonderful little *Franciscan Footlocker* that will fit out of the way subtly, yet gape a greeting every time you need it. A Sherwood Forest kind of security.

Last But Not Least—Special Appendix

4
Medium-Sized Secret Places

Vacant heart, and hand, and eye,
Easy live and quiet die.
                              —SCOTT

IT HAS BEEN SAID THAT THIS LAND IS YOUR LAND
while at the same time this land is my land. Where do you keep
yours? When you start getting a little stock on the hoof, you
start thinking about green pastures and medium-sized secrets.
Middle-class people tend to have middling things to hide. No
reason to be ashamed of that.

My most prized possessions are medium sized. Even my car.
It's easier to drive down the middle of any road. I think the
tastiest part of an apple pie is in the core. The center of a circle
is the whole point. Do you see the intoxication that the liberation
from *small* creates? As into a wind-swept glade, lost in fall sun-
shine, faunlike we enter the refreshing spaces afforded by medium-sized secret compartments.

I shouldn't have to mention that the fine line between small
and medium requires expert measurement. For example, the
Franciscan Footlocker discussed at the end of the previous chapter. You could make three such compartments side by side and
have a medium-sized open space available from the combination.
In the real world, nothing is fixed. Permutations proliferate.
Everything changes. Just as hidey holes are ever adaptable.

I can think of another good example of a multiplied hidey hole. It was one I built in a renovated brownstone in Greenwich Village. It was on one of those too-nice streets with well-kept but forbidding four story structures narrowly mashed together. Gardens and trees hid behind the houses in the center of each block. The brick landmark exterior of this particular house had been sandblasted and refurbished. The inside was another story, however. It had been completely altered to a garish modern design. The beams were absent. Brick walls were painted white. Gas pseudofire glowed in the fireplace niches. Oblique rectangles crying "Art" hung on the walls. Each small floor of the house was a carbon copy in a different color. Blue and red stripes on the wall followed you up the stairway. The steps themselves were newly carpeted in a shaggy hairbone pattern.

The customer, I soon discovered, was ahead of his time. He wore a scintillating shirt, opened to reveal his chest hair, and suede britches, bell bottomed and brushed. He was intense, saying things like, "I understand. I understand." He then proceeded to talk of his career in advertising. He talked of the celebrities he had loved, hardly sweating. The ads he had written. His two-thousand-dollar tooth and how it was worth it. He wanted me to adore his style, a jungle cat in the giant terrarium of life. I raised the corners of my mouth and finally got the information I needed to find a hiding place for him.

With celestial white spread amply over the whole apartment, there weren't many possibilities for my normal hidey hole approaches. This wasn't heaven. It was limbo, the place where pink drippy things go to ooze out a wait for eternity. It was like a new gas station's toilet, clean, to be sure, a gleaming white-and-chrome place that you were supposed to trust. It said sophistication, genius, gallery for myself, hang me in your memory, I'm lovely. The guy's eyes wavered as though floating in fluid, slopping back and forth, intent nevertheless, but he was riding some kind of pills.

"Well, what do-ya-think? What can you do, do for me?"

"Mr. F.," I said, "as my personal master, Henry James, did often say, 'I have just the thing.'

"You realize, don't you, that your shaggy-dog stairs are a design inspiration. It's the cogent contrast between warm and soft and bright and cold, do you know what I mean? And besides being in exquisite taste, your stairs offer a perfect place for a medium-sized secret compartment."

He bent over at the waist and looked at his stairsteps. "Yeah," he said. "I guess so. I've seen those in movies."

"Yes," I said. "I've seen that sort as well. But the compartment I build avoids that cliché."

He nodded at that. It didn't take long for him to grasp the principle, but what he then said astounded me. "How much to make three of them all together?"

Though it had never occurred to me before, it was clear that this was another hidey hole that could be enlarged by grouping. Mr. F. soon got what he wanted, and I went away with even fonder regard for this simple compartment.

THE KICKER

All steps cover an area of dead space. Some houses have regular little storage rooms under there. Others kill the space by closing it off completely. In any event, the back panel of each step, the kickboard, can serve as a door to hidden space. Many stairways, like Mr. F.'s, have only the steps themselves carpeted with the rear kickboard painted. This is ideal for our purposes. Fully carpeted stairs won't work. Not unless you recarpet so that each step top is done separately from the face/kickboards. This can be accomplished with little difficulty, and it gives the appearance of a top-to-bottom carpet strip.

The initial challenge is to remove the designated kickboard from the stable structure of the stairs. This may require crowbar prying, drilling and cutting, and a terrible mutilation of the board. Fear not. You can replace the old board and cover it with the same amount of paint as the other kickboards in the stairway. By any means, remove that board and prepare your new piece, the kicker door. Align and examine it. Does it fit perfectly? It must be chaste of suspicion.

The door itself can function in one of several ways. I explain here the up-and-in opening fulcrum approach, where the bottom of the panel pushes in and up. This works superbly with common situations you'll encounter. The pullout approach is another possibility. The principles of both of these are rather simple, merely depending on the kind of fasteners you use, those explained in Chapter 7.

The Kicker

You may have to do some masquerading under the steps themselves if there is a ready access through a door to that area. We wouldn't want the exterminator to stumble over your hidden stamp collection, would we? This concealment is usually nothing more involved than nailing up some sheeting or plywood to block off a portion of the underside of the stairs in some natural-seeming motif. (See also *Understep Safe.*)

IN THE BEAM

For those who walk the straight and narrow, following the success ascension, there is usually a romantic yearning for an abode in an idyll with age-darkened wood beams across the ceilings. Maybe it's Tudor X signatures you crave, or Romanesque dungeons underfoot. But probably the wood beams resting overhead are the dominant motif and aesthetic of your dream. You are in your castle, Mr. D., pickets guard your points.

Dick Nixon had wood-beamed ceilings. Stan Musial, Franz Kafka, and Dominick XIV preceded him, so there must be something to it. People love them simply because they are a natural luxury in a dwelling unit. Are you already a lucky success with timber beams in your ceilings or on your walls? Bravo! or Brava! However, if you're still an aspirant, waiting at life's pleasure door, there's no reason to wait any longer. You too can add the decorous solidity of beams in your very own home.

The tried and true heavy traditional wood beam is the ideal naturally. Who prefers plastic cups to a flow-lined glass? Few. Likewise with wood beams. Unfortunately, heavy structural ceiling beams are not very practical for the *In the Beam* secret compartments. Ceiling beams fashioned out of a "U" shape of two-inch boards are manageable, however.

If you must, you can buy lightweight foam pseudobeams, which are painted and scarred so realistically on the outside that upon first entering a door your peripheral vision tells you they're real.

Also consider side beams along walls. These are especially easy to handle, and I recommend them as first choices, if they aren't structural, simply because they're easier to get at. You may also add wall beams to a room with or without overhead ones.

In any approach, the hidey hole appears in the beam itself

from the backside or behind it in the wall. The primary problem is to cut the beam to fit in place, a perfect match for all similar beams in the ceiling or on the wall. You may have to rasp and sand one end so that it will fit snugly with just enough margin to permit it to swing in and out of place. One end of the beam will be anchored in place with a hinging device. The illustration points out typical hinge- and fastening-device locations. Another variety of this idea would be to place hinge devices along one side with the fasteners opposite, to thus swing the beam open sideways. This is only practical with wall beams and short lengths of ceiling beams. (Also see *Pilaster*.)

THE WINE COFFIN

Board designs and patterns on walls, as in the Tudor mode, work very well for secret compartment concealment. Usually these boards are painted or stained dark to contrast with the light wall. Calling attention to themselves so brazenly, the boards gain anonymity in their greater design. Pick one part, one little bottle-sized board, and put a secret spot there.

As you discovered with the *Closet King* and the *Mellors Model*, the board-hinging-away-from-the-wall approach is a rather simple one after you get the knack of the nook. Using Tudor board decor on your wall, you may uncover space as large as six feet long and six inches high. The depth, of course, will be determined by the wall, fitting in among the studs. The hinge or fastening choices here are numerous. This hidey hole weathers well, and if you wish, it will provide ample security for that rare vintage wine you're saving for your promotion.

SURREPTITIOUS SILL

Where does the enemy lurk? Over there. And where is the burglar? At the window. That's where he tramples the phlox, contorting his eye to fit through the slight crack in your curtains. And what does he see? He sees you stripping for bed, or packing for a weekend in the mountains. But already you have made a fool of him. Already he's overlooking the windowsill, peering through the frame at the innards of your house. To the ferret-lobed lucre eater, the window is synonymous with outside: he wants in. If you have a *Surreptitious Sill* under your window, already you will have fooled him, crisscrossed his craving eyes.

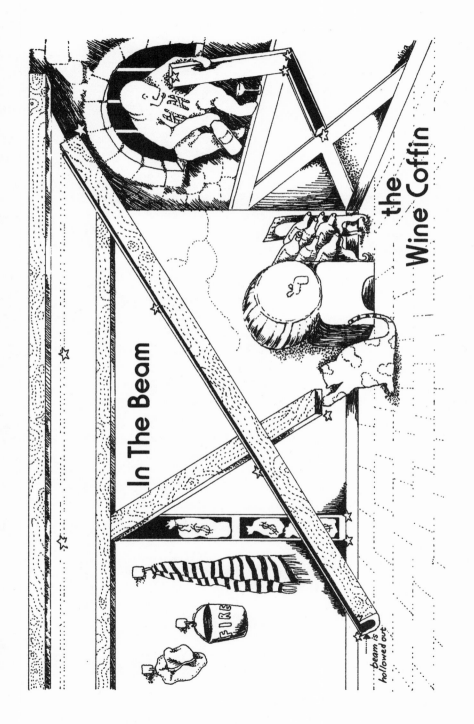

In The Beam

the Wine Coffin

FIRE

beam is hollowed out

Surreptitious Sill

This is not an easy carpentry job. You will probably have to put in a new window frame, or at least rebuild the windowsill and moldings, so this hidey hole is a good one to integrate into a house under construction. If you're building a new home, don't you dare "leave everything to the builder." Besides losing artistic control over your future living environment, it'll cost you more. Get involved. Wake those workmen up, those big hairy pussy cats. Kick 'em in the butt. You'll have a house done quicker, cheaper, and more in your own image. In the bargain, you might make some friends and learn something.

For the person who is about to grasp hold of the dream, "building your own home," this is a wonderfully opportune meeting. Hopefully, you'll be able to take several ideas from this book for your Future Home. I understand there are Future Homers' organizations in many cities now, creeping closer every day. And nothing could better symbolize their clear thinking and farsightedness than a *Surreptitious Sill* hidey hole. Good luck, you hear.

If you're capable of working up a *Surreptitious Sill*, you can already visualize each of the pieces of wood that go into making a window. The mere name of the hidey hole already clues you in to what is involved. The windowsill. That board that serves as a shelf at the bottom of the window. When the sill is removed you are granted a generous hunk of wall space between the studs. Most windows give you at least two feet of width, all access. Since this occurs several feet off the floor, all of that depth inside the wall is yours, to fill with what you will.

Quite frankly, I fear for your windowsill board. Your best bet may be to replace it after it is damaged beyond repair in removal. A replica sill can probably be found or one can be created by a woodcraftsman with his special tools. I know you'd like to save the window. But sometimes there's nothing you can do about it. In which case, a new window might look nice where that old one was. That's right. Yank that old window out and put in a new one, a bigger one. You'll not only get more sunlight, but you'll have more wall to hide in. Sounds like a contradiction, doesn't it?

The actual applications you'll be employing here are similar to the *Book Basement* and the *Mellors Model*. You can rest your elbows there while you lean, chin in hand, and stare at your horizon, dreaming up adventures involving you and your *Surreptitious Sill* hidey hole.

ACOUSTICAL PANEL

This is a boring secret compartment so I'll try to get it over with as quickly as possible. It's really cheap. Even nuns can afford this one. They can, that is, if they can afford to put in a new ceiling, a relatively inexpensive task. Certainly inexpensive compared to paying for the city's daily breadline soup pot.

You've seen this sort of ceiling before. It is the kind of thing they use to make dropped ceilings these days in restaurants and renovated rooms. It features a metal frame hanging from the real ceiling. Acoustical panels then rest on the metal frame. They are available in various sizes, but all have one thing in common—they rest in place in the frame by gravity. All that is necessary to reach the dead space hidden behind the dropped ceiling is to stand on a chair and push a panel up and to the side. The space presented to you depends on how much area you have closed off. If you have one of those wonderful old houses with mammoth ceilings, you could even close off a whole secret room up there. You could hold crap games up there or peek down at the people below, giggling with satisfaction.

This entry method to a secret space is very high risk. A Secretary of State wouldn't trust it. But if you've fallen in love with it and simply must have it, you could do this. Use magnet fasteners on the movable panel and glue all of the other panels into place. That cuts down the odds against Noseys.

CEILING TILE TUCKAWAY

Ceiling tile are as American as bread and butter. There are ceiling tile of diverse descriptions available. There are holes in some to deaden sound; others have decorator patterns or come in plain old white. I wouldn't recommend using the latter in conjunction with a *Ceiling Tile Tuckaway* since finger marks could compromise you.

The actual installation of ceiling tile is an easy matter. The most important state is the preparation. You must draw lines on the ceiling that will guide you in laying the tile straight. These lines have to be perfectly parallel to the walls. A chalk line comes in handy for this sort of thing, but you can also measure over from a sidewall and construct your straight line that way. Only two or three such lines are necessary in an average-sized room—

Acoustical Panel

Ceiling Tile
Tuckaway

Understep Safe

simply a reference point as you affix the tile to make sure you are keeping the rows regular. Better than a hammer, a stapling gun is a quick and efficient means of fastening. But it doesn't work well with plaster ceilings. Straight rows of wood strips, firmly nailed to the ceiling, will aid you over such hurdles. The tile is then stapled to the strips. Your local retail dealer will be able to help you with any questions you might have.

Before you complete the tile installation, you must choose the hidey-hole site. It will nestle behind one tile, preferably toward a corner of the room. A hole will have to be hollowed out of the ceiling, removing plaster and wood. Be careful not to interfere with any electrical lines, plumbing, or structural beams you might encounter.

Once the tile are in place around the hole you have created it is time to install the final unit, the door to your compartment. Chapter 7 will show you the spring hinge, magnet fasteners, and other fastening devices. If you keep your hands clean, not to mention your nose, no trace of your visits to the *Ceiling Tile Tuckaway* will remain.

UNDERSTEP SAFE

The good old houses always had a little room under the stairs. It was a closet or a storage area or the maid's nook, but it was always characterized by a unique shape. As an ill-adjusted child seeking mental health in fantasy, you could climb under there and pretend you were a troll waiting for the heavy footfall that would guarantee a high protein meal. Nowadays, people are less inclined in this direction. Just as psychology-fixated Americans espouse openness and honesty at the expense of closed mouths and silent prayer, so also do modern builders leave open expanses under stairs. Or even worse, they seal the space up with plasterboard and fast-drying paint. Still, there's hope for stair owners. If you have a little room under your mounting path to the boudoir, or are willing to make one there, the *Understep Safe* is awaiting your approval.

The first time I built this secret compartment it was for a businessman who wanted to hide a small safe in his home, consequently the name. The three-or-four-foot-deep space under the lowest steps is where we are going to concentrate. Ordinarily, this is an out-of-the-way dirty place that no one has a good use for. It is only reasonable that a homeowner would close that area off with shelves. I prefer shelves two to four inches deep. These can be used to store cleaning solutions, paints, and the like. Such a storage area looks natural and, like housework, is uninviting to the observer.

You will have to design the shelf suitable to your specific situation. But the task is simple, actually a larger version of the *Spice Nook* described in Chapter 2. The most important thing is that the shelf fit snugly top and bottom and with an inch or so crack on the side. There must be a plywood back to the shelf so no one can see into the hidden space. Once the shelf is built and fitted, hinge one side so that it will swing open and closed. This completed, choose fastening devices for the other side so the shelf, when closed, will snap firmly in place.

There are obvious and visible cracks running around the outsides of the shelf. Cover these with removable molding as explained in Chapter 7. Suddenly it dawns on you that the newly constructed shelf stands out from the rest of the area under the stairs like a walnut on a putting green. You might want to paint everything a uniform color. I would not recommend drawing attention to the shelves with careful stain and finishing. Considering the location, it would be better to bang up the shelves a bit and cover them with a cheap discoloring varnish. Maybe spill a little paint on one of the shelves to show that it has been there doing dirty work for years.

Behind the shelves, under those lower steps, you can be as lavish as the space permits. Carpeting is nice. Maybe a Japanese TV and an ice cooler of beer. Any time the kids get to be too much, you can climb under there and hide. Or if you have fugitive friends, you might find that your house is more popular than ever before.

CUPBOARD ENCLOSURE

Apartment dwellers live among all varieties of architectural quirks. There are columns and corners at unexpected junctures, kitchens crammed into odd quarters, and occasional vents and grills nestling near the ceiling. You've seen those square grills in windowless bathrooms, venting noxious odors from floor upon floor. Similarly, kitchens often have such grill plates covering the vents. It's not nearly as classy as a proper ventilation fan system,

Cupboard Enclosure

entrance grill

Nina

but it is functional in a traditional way nonetheless. Since these grills are common, it would not be out of place to add one to your abode, if you don't have one to make use of already. A plausible location can be found in the upper regions of your walls permitting you a small secret place. But for more space, I prefer the following approach.

Do you have kitchen cabinets hung on the walls with a foot or so of open space above them to the ceiling? Wasted space, right? You put odd-size utensils up there, or useless kitchen gifts from relatives. Why not enclose that space and use it for concealment? You can frame it in, using plywood, plasterboard, or plaster, but you will have to do a smooth job on this or it won't look like an original structure. When closing in the space, allow for the thickness of plaster so that the entire construct is flush with the sides of the cupboard. The important stage is cutting out a hole for the grill plate to fit over. This should be on the side most plausible for ventilating the stove area.

Once constructed, repaint the entire kitchen or else come up with some fancy wallpaper or two-tone paint job to make the decor blend. All of the hidden space behind the grill should be painted black to make it look dark and ventlike. If you wish, you can install a simple hinged panel inside the compartment to conceal some of the space and further confound intruders. Then fashion false screws for the grill plate and choose a magnet-fastening device or some other alternative in good old Chapter 7.

THE PLATO PANEL

If you recall our lengthy discussion of secret panels in Chapter 2, you'll have the needed techniques to approach the *Plato Panel*. It is an excellent compartment to use in conjunction with *Wall Expansion,* which is explained in Special Appendix, an approach I heartily recommend. It gives you added depth behind the compartment panel, for easier access and storage.

The *Plato Panel* is simply a secret panel at the back of a bookcase. Now, there are bookcases and there are bookcases. What we're discussing here is not the nickel-and-dime variety which is perfectly suitable for the *Book Basement*. No. This requires more ambition. It's like the difference between oranges and kiwi fruit, apples and apple pie, a city councilman and a senator.

To be more specific, you have to sweat, as Plato did when he took his last drink thinking of Socrates.

What you will need is a substantial bookcase with a wood back to it that's firmly fastened to the wall. The ideal here would be one of those creatively wrought wall-unit compositions with multi-sized shelves—a unit that can graciously hold books and such things as magazines, records, sound equipment, and tarnished trophies. By designing the unit yourself, you'll be able to create confusion in the observers' minds by varying the size and shape of each shelf opening. A by-product is that you can create the most conveniently sized location for the *Plato Panel* while camouflaging it among the irregular diversity of shelves.

Viewed from the front, the bookcase looks solid, and any normal-thinking person would assume that the wood back to the unit is of one piece. This proves the adage "normal thinking leads not up nor down but round and round." By your own individualistic hand, you will cut out one section of the backing behind your chosen shelf. Now replace it with an undamaged panel of like wood. This will be your hinged and movable secret panel. After referring to the *Elementary Secret Panel* in Chapter 2, you'll select your hinge and fastening method from Chapter 7. Once again, your bookshelf unit will look solid and of a piece. No one will suspect that one part of that seemingly solid back will yield to the knowing hand. It's the nicest way I know to be pushy.

FALSE CORNER FURRING

Picture this. The night is dark in the apartment high above Manhattan's fashionable East Side. Diffused city light slats in through the venetian blinds. The corners of the apartment are dark and quiet. She stands terrified in a corner, the fuses blown. Only Harry knows about that. Not skinny, not fat, she blends into the corner darkness well. Only her many-jeweled house necklace catches the zebra light occasionally as she trembles. The taxis hum by on the avenue below and just short feet away delicate clicks in the keyhole announce an arriving criminal. Her mouth is open like fish death. The door opens.

The burglar's teeth shine in the avenue light as he dance-shuffles and hand-muffles the door closed behind him. Um. Um. It is some apartment. He has to step up to mount the carpet. He knows right where to go. To the jewelry case by the window.

It has been left open spilling brooches and bracelets in a cascading flash of diamond chunks. He knows right where to go.

He takes long fluid strides across the room. She can almost feel the intense rhythmical heat of his muscle flow. Such a build he has. Why, he could kill her with one hand. She squeezes her buttocks tight into the corner and quivers in place, her eyes as wide as Rocky Mountain oysters. He wears tight pants. She wonders where he is going to put her precious ones that he now fondles in his hands. He reaches into a back pocket and removes a small plastic garbage bag, black. In handfuls he roughly handles her treasures, smacking them against the bottom of the black bag, twisty at the top, and he is out the door, gone.

Immediately she falls into a limp posture and bemoans her loss. A life's worth of acquisitions. Gone. What will Harry say?

But what she doesn't know is that the man works for Harry. Does all of Harry's dirty work. And Harry needs cash. The fastest way to get it is to steal his wife's jewels, pay off the man with as little as possible, and collect the insurance.

Now, all of this wouldn't have happened, of course, if Harry's wife had a hidey hole. He is never at home and besides he has his own bedroom, so she could get a workman in her bedroom any time she wanted, and she could have a secret place constructed as invisible as she was the night of the crime. On the same spot where she stood, she could create a corner in a corner. She could false corner fur.

False Corner Furring is simply the process by which a normal 90-degree room corner is suddenly visited by a pillar, a structural-seeming projection into the room, ceiling to floor. A stranger would look at it and yawn. Just another odd corner in a random-shaped apartment. No doubt it is a cement pillar in there supporting the apartment building. Or maybe plumbing flushes behind that normal-looking projection of wall. But no. You've fooled them. Have a laugh. That's not part of the wall. It's a false corner.

You're going to have to build a wall. If you are a rank neophyte, read *Carpentry* in Special Appendix. In addition, you will be nailing up a wall of wood paneling, like it or not. If you stop to think a moment, you will understand why. If you were to build a false corner and plaster it all over like all the other walls, it wouldn't be false. You wouldn't be able to get into it.

There are other ways you could create an entrance point in such a corner, but the one I choose to employ is the paneled wall. You can get by using that cheap, prefinished plywood that lumber dealers like to sell. But you know what I think about that.

The ruse technique is simple. You will panel one wall of the room and *one side* of the false corner. The latter will be the opening door to the compartment. You will leave the other side of the false construction to be plastered and appear like the wall it abuts. If you really want to, you can panel the entire false corner and still gain entrance to the dead space in the same manner. There is a crack at the projecting corner where the two faces of the false walls meet. This crack is the opening point to the secret place. Hinges anchor the other side of this door. One entire side of the false corner will swing open. And once closed, a removable molding will fit over that telltale crack, hiding it from sight and suspicion. You may add an additional removable molding along the ceiling and a removable baseboard along the floor if you wish.

If you are using actual wall-panel boards as described in Chapter 2, *Elementary Secret Panel*, you will be able to alter this door-within-the-paneling technique to work for you, concealing inset wall space or a false closet wall.

INSET WALL SPACE

Occasionally a house or apartment has an inset space in one of its walls. This may be due to architectural necessity or simply as a convenient location for shelves. The point in its favor is, by paneling that entire wall, making it a straight line, the inset wall space will disappear and no one will be the wiser. Tongue-and-groove paneling as previously mentioned works well in such an instance.

You must measure carefully as per usual. Construct the door to the secret place first. This will consist of several boards attached with crossing pieces screwed to the backs, out of sight. Once this is completed, make sure it fits the space perfectly. Next, nail the boards on either side of the inset wall space. One of these will serve as the anchor mount for your hinges and the other will provide the seat for the fastening devices as described in Chapter 7. The cracks that appear between the fixed wall-panel boards and the movable door of paneling must not be

False Corner Furring

paneling

molding

studs
false wall

Inset Wall Space

cedar boards

False Closet Back

conspicuous. You have the choice of making your panel door swing inward or out into the room. To open outward, you will need a means of gaining purchase to pull the door open. Read the discussion of *Picks* in Chapter 7. Once you have your door of paneling mounted and functional, you may proceed to nail on the remaining wall-paneling boards. A removable ceiling molding and baseboard will add a finishing touch. Now is the time when you truly begin to see what you have wrought. The entire wall is attractive wood. Your furniture suddenly looks more expensive. Your wife or husband exclaims in falsetto. You are flushed with pride.

FALSE CLOSET WALL

The same technique can be employed in constructing a false closet wall. You should have a roomy closet to work with for starters. One in which six inches or a foot of concealed space at the back will not be missed. To make it plausible for wood paneling to appear in your closet, use sweet-smelling cedar boards. Your clothes will smile, and moths will flee in terror from the mellow aroma. Don't be surprised if you decide to throw out the clothes and put an easy chair in the closet, converting it to a private reading room. Have you ever read a book while sniffing cedar? It alerts you to nuance.

You Can't Go Wrong at Special Appendix

5
Big Secret Places

There is nothing as great
As man's love of man,
But for his largesse of fear.
—ANONYMOUS

THE LAST SECRET COMPARTMENT I EVER BUILT FOR pay was the most unusual. I had to drive for an hour north of New York City on a rainy night. Already I felt as if the job weren't worth it. But the man had been very positive on the phone, had guaranteed my expenses, and he claimed to live in a mansion formerly owned by Jackie Gleason. Away I went, but it was raining and I felt shivers touching my spine.

The driveway wound through dark trees. Wet leaves stuck to my windshield. There were few lights on in the bulky building that loomed before me. A butler ushered me in. My host sat in a wheelchair facing away from me, watching the snap and crackle of the fireplace.

"Good evening," his baritone voice toned as he spun the chair around to face me. His face was a shock. It was as though a sick cartoonist had smeared nauseous colors on a canvas with a blunt knife. Some terrible accident had befallen the man, and the plastic surgeon had been hard pressed to maintain even the semblance of a face. "Don't be embarrassed," he said, sparkling a ring finger at me. Or rather the ring sparkled, on the stub of the ring finger of his right hand. "War wounds. I'm sure you understand."

I got the feeling he was looking at my long hair, as he said it almost sarcastically. But I couldn't be sure of that. There was no expression identifiable on that hideous face. As a matter of fact, the face didn't even reveal what war it was erased in. His hairy arms were muscled, but they could have been twenty-five years old or a well-preserved fifty. He did have to use them all the time with his wheelchair. A rich war veteran. How do you figure that one, I wondered.

"In case you're wondering," he said psychically, "my father was in munitions." I couldn't believe he was saying it. The irony. The irony.

He led me around the downstairs rooms as we discussed his needs. He wanted a large secret space. Large enough for him to wheel his chair into, is the way he described it. He didn't explain why he wanted to do such a thing, and I ceased caring as I began examining the immense house around me.

"And the upstairs?" I asked.

"I don't go up there. I leave it to the servants and the rats." There was a flicker of movement along the edges of his mouth hole. I had kept my eyes for the most part averted. Suddenly I realized he had been watching me intently since I came in. Now, I felt I had to get away from him. I knew it. He obliged me and returned to stare into his fieldstone fireplace. I wandered the first floor again.

The house was revisionist rococo in design. Fluted pilasters climbed walls at unlikely places. Gingerbread moldings near the ceiling seemed to be rows of perched spectators watching. Gothic arches convoluted over doorways. Checkerboard tile was as frequent as carpeting on the floors. My mind went back. Fluted pilasters. I remembered my research at the public library. In the late sixteenth century and early seventeenth century, priests were returning to England to reestablish Catholicism. Unfortunately underground secret Mass centers were necessary, and often a secret place for a fugitive priest was needed. *Hide Makers*, as they were called, were at a premium. They preferred to adapt some existing feature. They seldom let light fall on the secret location: backs of cupboards, movable floorboards, blackened chimney brick.

The best known hide maker was Nicholas Owen in Worcester and Warwickshire. He often made double hides, the second being the escape shaft. He strived to use different approaches each time, and never talked, even when he was seized after the Gunpowder Plot and tortured for his secrets. Look it up at your nearest good library. Fascinating.

The one secret entrance that most entranced me from reading about this period was Nicholas Owen's pilaster. He had a movable pilaster as an entrance to a secret passageway. Back again in the twentieth century I looked at the gross grand architecture that surrounded me. All of the pilasters were made of wood. Marble occurred only in the arches and actual columns found in the entrance hall of the house. I realized that I could make Nick Owen's secret place. Bring a smile to his powdered face.

I didn't have much trouble finding an out-of-the-way pilaster on the opposite side of a wall from a closet. You can wheel a chair into a closet. I had to summon help on this particular job since the pilaster was of considerable size and weight. With the large fee my host agreed to pay me, I didn't come out too badly on the deal. I hired a carpenter friend who knew what he was doing in such a setting.

PILASTER

I anticipate carping from the gallery. Who wants to build a *Pilaster* secret compartment, the dubious among you ask; you can't even afford plaster. But pause a moment. Never hasten to discard an idea just because it is alien. Remember how we used to hate the Red Chinese? Remember the *In the Beam* hidey holes in the last chapter? What is that illustrated wood wall beam but a simple pilaster? If it is a support beam, that's one thing. If it is nonfunctional, it is the equivalent of a pilaster. Also, pilasterlike support protrusions occur in cement block walls in basements. Often these are framed in, maintaining their shape when such a wall is paneled with plywood. Think about it. It is a very structural appearing construction that you can add to a naked basement wall. And, with a little design creativity, you could, like

Pilaster

Nina

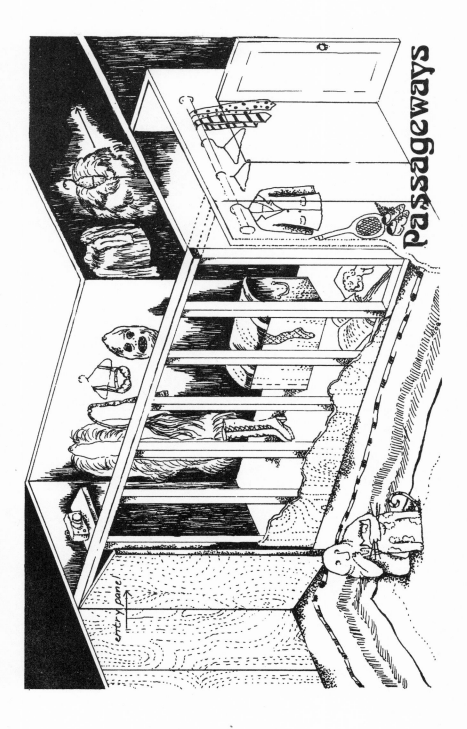

False Corner Furring, utilize such an approach on normal upstairs walls.

It should be obvious then that a genuine pilaster, wall beam, or false pilaster-type construct of any plausible design can be utilized to conceal a great deal of space. It can be a doorway to a mere wall compartment or an entire chamber. So, consider the possibilities of your house from basement to attic before discarding this approach to secret doors.

The method of attachment is similar in all cases. One side of the pilaster structure is hinged; the other has fastening devices that allow it to snap closed. When properly constructed, it would take a very strong pull to release the fasteners and open the pilaster/door. This in itself is probably all the security one would need. People don't go around houses pulling on protrusions and corners. Of course a secret locking device can be conjured that will keep the pilaster firmly in place until knowledgeably released. You know now where to find that information.

People don't expect walls to be straight. They're used to protrusions into every aspect of their lives. Your biggest worry is finding a way to make a large space behind your secret door. The previously discussed veteran afforded me a large house in which to locate an ideal spot, a closet I could break through to from the rear. I then closed off the regular closet door and plastered the wall up. The house was large enough that no one would question what happened to the space the closet occupied. You may not have such ideal circumstances. But if you walk around your abode scrutinizing space relations as would a suspicious stranger, you may find that you too can close off a closet, or the back of a closet, or false corner fur with an entrance from the back through the original wall. When you move up to large secret spaces, you are also moving up the ladder of challenge. When the going gets tough, the smart take time to think about it. I've always found a solution waiting. So will you. If you can handle it, you might like to use your pilaster as an entrance to a passageway, just like old Nick Owen.

PASSAGEWAYS

If you live in a bungalow, there's no sense dreaming about creating labyrinthian secret passageways in which to spirit your money away from bill collectors. Unfortunately, you have to have a large or at least complex house to accommodate the hidden space required for passageways.

For example, here is what would be required in a very minimal secret passage structure. You could have a false furred corner, or a false closet back inside which a hole is opened straight down through the floor for quick secret access to the basement. Or you could mount a ladder there to sneak up into the attic. At either end of such a passageway, you would have to shield the traveling space and make a secret exit point. In the basement you could descend inside what appeared to be a square support pillar and exit through a door in the wood paneling the pillar is sheathed with. You get the idea. I will give you ample approaches to mull over. The problem is hiding the space of the passageway. In old houses this is less difficult than with modern homes. Walls are thicker, rooms more plentiful and commodious; orientation and fixation on space relationships are not as simple for the casual visitor or criminal. The same is true with apartments. More generously spaced apartments offer possibilities small ones do not.

Obviously, the ingredients of your passageway construction will be totally unique, the problems all your own. The question of why you would even want a secret path can be answered only by you. Consequently for purposes of illustration and by way of jogging your imagination for your particular task, I've chosen to show a simple technique that will provide some common applications.

The illustration shows you how one end of a room can be closed off with a false wall. In this case we use wood paneling to camouflage the entrance point. You could, of course, plaster the wall and use some other entrance device. The secret passage here provides both a secret hiding space in and of itself and leads to a hole knocked through the original wall and off into your particular dark distance. To be more direct, you could employ false corner furring right in front of the hole in the wall. But it would be less exciting, wouldn't it? Notice how the passageway passes behind a closet back. Should you desire, you could contrive a hole through that wall so that on a given occasion you could flee one room into your secret passageway, climb into the closet and when the coast is clear, open the door and escape.

Having a closet appear in such a location, as you can see,

The Gothic Wall

helps conceal the fact that a chunk of the main room has been closed off behind the new wall. Such considerations are important if you don't want to hear your father-in-law someday ask, "Say, isn't there something funny about that wall?"

Passageways that incorporate exchange of floor levels are especially pleasing. Each time you close your secret door behind you and make your way toward your destination, you have the satisfaction that comes from pulling one over on somebody. You can even contrive peepholes and peep, spending hours hidden inside your wall. You can hide people there and they'll have room enough to exercise while they're waiting for you to let them out.

The ultimate in passageway building, naturally, is in the challenge of integrating one in a house under construction. Find an architect you can trust if you really want to get sophisticated. In a new house as with newly met friends, you can conceal all manner of things.

THE GOTHIC WALL

The American Gothic is an emotion. It strikes some like a madness and others with design. Grant Wood memorialized an Iowa pitchfork. Our forefathers slept in graveyards during the Revolution, awakening to feel damp mist on the fieldstones like shot around them. Today our mothers and daughters flee raping shadows through paperbacked corridors of Victorian manses, repeating the journey after each new escape. There is Afro-American Gothic, fashioned under our very corn-yellow eyes, a living embodiment of guilt in our brick and soot and steel jungles. Gothic is as Gothic does, and we have a corner on the market.

This right-thinking secret compartment, the *Gothic Wall*, may become your symbol. You can fashion your own identity on its face, and thus live looking at yourself in the walls surrounding you. The *Gothic Wall* is a design you can create to look spare and modern in bright enamel lines, or you can cover it with rich fabric, lush in its sense of decadent age.

This is a time consuming, but regal plan for opening large portions of wall for secret space. Essentially what it entails is a series of large plywood panels, as imbued with atmosphere as you desire to make them. The height of your ceilings and width of your room will determine the actual size of each panel. Measure and calculate so that a number of whole panels will cover your walls with a minimum of odd-shaped sections to ruin the symmetry. Naturally above and below windows will require specially shaped smaller panels of the same general design.

Cut all of your main panels to size. Use three-quarter-inch plywood, A-D grade. Paint the outer edges all around with a flat black paint. From the illustration you can see that there will be slightly smaller plywood panels, approximately an inch less on each side. These will be affixed centrally over the larger sheets of plywood. But before you do that, cover the smaller panels with the fabric you desire for a wall decoration. It can be expensive designer fabric, burlap, or you can even settle for paint, any color you wish. Frame around the outside edge of the smaller panel with 1 by 2s mitered at the corners. This is what adds class to the design. The wood frame finished with stain, clear, or painted will leave only a small portion of the black back panel visible. Measure carefully to center the two panels together, nail and/or screw. Once this is done you will have several big wall panels that only require attachment to the walls. You might as well put the permanently affixed panels up first so you can get a feel of the room.

In the space where the designated panel or panels will swing open to reveal the hiding area, do your destruction and construction work. Obviously these panels can conceal either large spaces of shelves between wall studs, passageways, or rooms. Once this is done, mount the movable panel or panels with hinges on one side and fasteners on the other. Chapter 7 will help you choose the method. Heavy hinges or a large number of smaller ones will be required. You might even add a caster at the backside of the swinging corner to help bear the weight.

Once in place and snapped shut, your walls will inflate your ego and flatter your taste. The slight black area visible in the space between each panel will be the highlighting factor and will at the same time conceal the joining cracks of both the permanent and movable panels.

There is something very traditional about the scope of the *Gothic Wall* panels. Their size recalls to mind grander times than our tricky-eyed present. They make one think of Cardinal's chambers in Inquisition splendor. Of country clubs before sullying enrollments disturbed their incest. Of bar cabinets and trophies,

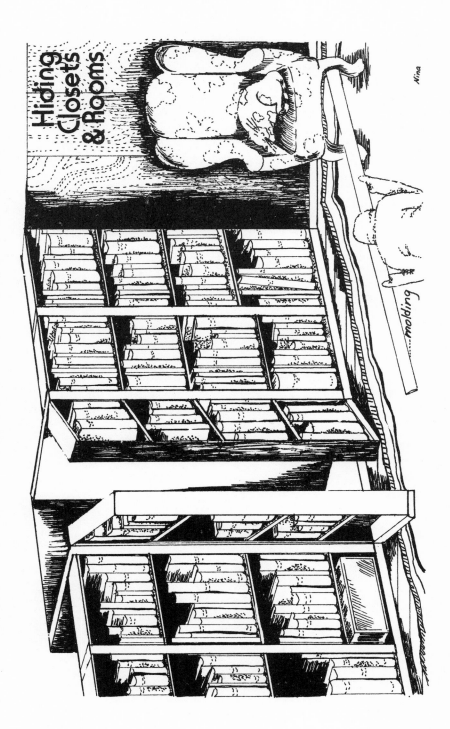

fireplaces and roasting red meat, dark shadows and the screaming night sounds of owls and snared rabbits. The *Gothic Wall* is a timeless remnant of history we can all clutch onto, opening our secrets.

HIDING CLOSETS AND ROOMS

There are many wall treatments that can be employed to hide a closet or a room. Those previously mentioned are *Wall Beam,* pilaster approaches, *False Corner Furring, False Closet Wall,* and the *Gothic Wall.* Coming up are the *Batten Wall Storehousing* technique and trapdoors, both discussed in Chapter 6, and the *Rustic Wall Treatment* in Special Appendix. The method I will detail here is the tried and true traditional movable bookcase.

I've touched upon the difficulties of plausibility created by hiding large spaces. Even casual visitors can sense a missing room in a simple and symmetrically laid-out house. Large houses with many rooms and a complicated layout obviously offer more to work with in this respect. But the easiest domicile of all in which to hide a room is an apartment. Apartments come in all sizes and shapes, one-room studios to three-floor multi-bedroom penthouses. Unless otherwise informed, who would know whether a bedroom disappeared or not? You really need this kind of optimum security for room hiding, or it isn't worth the effort. Only proceed if no one will suspect a room hidden behind your wall of bookcases.

You don't read books, you say? You don't have any in the house but for a couple of unread Reader's Digested Books with the yellow-striped spines? Shame on you. Weren't you spanked when you were young? Books are food, Francis Bacon once said. They're dynamizers, tranquilizers, exorcisors, and faithful friends. Books fight fever and fascism. By reading you might save thousands of dollars in psychiatric fees. Getting insights into your own life predicament. Be ahead of your time. Be the first on your block to give up television.

If you are going to use bookcase camouflage, you need to do something about getting books into your house if not your life. If you think you might read some of them, join a book club or two, cashing in on those introductory offers. There are cookbook clubs, sports book clubs, history, psychology, sex, mystery, occult,

Western, Eastern intellectual, science fiction, and bargain book clubs. But the biggest bargain of all if that's all you're looking for, is the thrift, flea, junk, and Salvation Army shop approach. You'll be able to pick up grosses of books inexpensively, fill up space, and insulate your wall of secret mystery. Start carrying a shopping bag with you when you take walks. Pick up books wherever you find them as long as no garbage still clings to the bindings.

Instead of putting books on all the shelves, you might want to show your modernity by filling blank spaces with small framed pictures, tasteful knickknacks, or dried flowers. You don't have to worry about calling attention to the shelves. Paint them red or hang fluorescent holy tapestries if you want. As long as the bookshelves look like a comfortable part of your house, secrecy will be maintained.

The construction and installation of this covert access are similar to the *Gothic Wall*. Instead of wall panel units, there will be units of bookshelves, two to four feet wide. As with the *Gothic Wall*, you will have to measure and determine the best width to keep the shelves uniform in size. These can be constructed of common pine or attractive hardwood. Eight-inch boards are preferable. There must be a back to each of the shelf units. This can be plywood or hardboard. The design option is yours but one necessary part of your planning will be the molding that fits between each unit of shelves.

Unlike a door, there is considerable depth to bookshelves. In order to have sufficient clearance for one or more of the bookcases to swing open, you will have to leave a small space between each of the shelf units. This will be hidden by a vertical molding nailed in place between the permanent units. Over the crucial cracks where the moving takes place, you will have to install removable moldings, using fastening devices.

Besides choosing from hinge devices listed in Chapter 7, I would recommend using heavy duty casters under the movable sections of shelf to help bear the weight without strain to your entire structure. Due to this considerable weight, the simpler fastening devices will suffice. It will take a hefty pull to swing the bookshelf door open, the kind of effort no one will do by accident unless a lot of people stumble with drinks at your place.

To balm justifiable paranoia, the *Nail Lock* device is simple to use with this secret compartment.

What you are concealing behind the bookcases could be just about anything. Closets fit well and are not easily missed. You might even put your rare and valuable books back there in a hidden row of bookshelves. If you've gone to all the trouble required to hide a large secret place, you must have a good use for it.

I propose a toast. Break open a bottle of wine or a can of beer or soda pop, pour it in one of your better glasses and join me. Clink. Here's to you and your secrets. May the calluses on your hands remain, a constant reminder of manual labor's satisfaction. And may we always maintain humility in the face of accomplishment.

Only 22 Pages to Special Appendix

6
Hiding in Your Second Home

And homeless near a thousand homes I stood,
And near a thousand tables pined and wanted food.
—WORDSWORTH

IF YOU AREN'T EMBARRASSED TO HAVE TWO OR MORE
homes while millions starve in dirt roadways the world over, this
chapter is for you. You can't be in both houses at once, that's for
sure, so it is only natural that you should feel anxious when you
leave one behind, unattended. Or maybe you can afford to pay
a watcher for your ski chalet, or the fishing cabin, or the house
on the dunes. But do you really think the watcher will always be
vigilant? You can't trust help these days. At base, the second home
is very problematical. What if organized crime elects you their
sucker-for-a-day? They could clean you out: the sound equipment, the appliances, even furniture. Are you going to let them
get away with that?

I'm reminded of the story about the Bold Weasels, a notorious Iowa gang of the nineteen fifties. I was only a tad then,
living in a small rural town watching kittens being born and
using cow-pies for bases. Aside from Robin Hood, the Bold
Weasels were my initiation into the world of thievery. Every
week an even larger headline would proclaim another poor farmer
fleeced.

The *modus operandi* was simple. The Weasels waited until a farmhouse was unattended, using a telescope for long-range observation. Then they boldly drove into the farmer's yard with their foul-smelling livestock truck and proceeded to load it with all items of value. Sometimes there was room to squeeze a suckling calf or a few hogs in the back.

Town Marshall Pogey finally apprehended the varmints, a blond trucker named Weasel and his two hefty daughters who hailed from Illinois. They regularly drove their livestock truck full of goodies to Chicago and there received good money for the antique furniture. The more mundane items such as television sets were fenced through a ghetto outlet.

There is a lesson to be learned here. A house unattended is a house unprotected. Obviously a hidey hole would be useful for the two-home owner. But with a house full of possessions left for long periods of time, you really need subterfuge on a large scale. I can recommend some approaches.

If you have just acquired the second home, or if you are building, avoid using valuable furnishings. Modern built-in units are the shrewdest approach. The most a crook can do then is to deface them with unsavory graffiti.

It is definitely a good idea to construct a decoy hiding place in your second home. A trapdoor under a rug, a shoddily constructed hidey hole or some other nook stuffed with a few semi-valuable items. If criminals do cross your threshold, they'll be thrown off by finding the decoy and will not begin to suspect your more ambitious secret compartment.

WALL STOREHOUSING

We've talked about using some of that dead space between wall studs. But when you are discussing hiding records, books, electrical appliances, liquor, Tiffany lamps, gun collections, sports and camera equipment, along with canned provisions and cat litter, then we're discussing huge amounts of space. With such quantities of vulnerable possessions, it would behoove us to use one or more entire walls for secret storage. You might want to employ *Wall Expansion* on the selected wall as explained in Special Appendix.

There is a variety of methods for gaining entrance to the hidden space. The basic idea is to have a wall that opens up. The

Gothic Wall explained in Chapter 5 would work here. Also a very Rustic Paneling motif is explained in Special Appendix. But an approach well in keeping with the vacation home conceit is the *Barn Board and Batten* technique, as can be seen in the illustration. Popularized in barn construction of the last century, thrifty boards and battens are found as the exterior of many a happy Midwest home. It is also used for rumpus-room paneling, for inexpensive bar and restaurant atmosphere, and there's no reason why you shouldn't get in on such a good thing.

First, the construction of the solid board and batten walls. Take ten- or twelve-inch-wide boards, sanded or rough, cut to fit vertically from floor to ceiling. Nail in place butted against each other across the wall. To cover the horizontal crack along the ceiling and the floor, nail moldings or simple 1 by 4s in place along the length of the wall. Done? Fast! Looks like the paneled wall we were discussing in Chapter 2, doesn't it? Now, cut 1 by 2 batten strips to fit and nail over the cracks between each of the wide vertical boards.

Having completed one or more solid walls in this fashion, you can readily see how you can use a batten to hide a junction crack between two portions of a wall, at least one of which moves. The batten covers the crack in the same way between all the boards. Again we are creating the mesmerizing effect of repetition. All of the boards and all of the battens look alike, just like rush-hour people.

Now comes the hard part, constructing the false wall that will swing open. Cut the boards, battens, and molding as if you were going to construct another permanent wall. You will have to measure carefully and determine the exact width of the movable section of the wall. Lay the boards out in perfect alignment side by side on the floor. Tie them together, using the old farmer's "Z" crossing pieces (as illustrated) screwed into each of the wallboards. The "Z" is what holds the boards together making a wall section that will be your door. You've seen the same arrangement in your neighbors' barn doors or while leaving antique shops. You may also employ a plywood sheet for this purpose.

Turn the wall section over and nail the battens in place over the cracks. Do not attach the ceiling or floor moldings yet. If you want to see how you're doing, lean the wall section in place, covering the soon-to-be-secret place. Looks good, doesn't it? You

Ḥiding In Your Second Ḥome

Boards

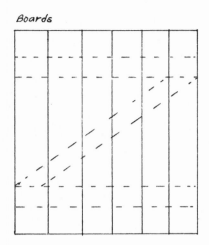

Over·lapping batten strip

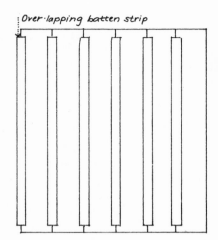

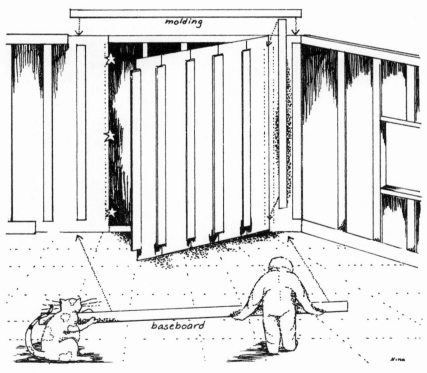

molding

baseboard

measured wrong? Now is the time to make any adjustments. Your wall must fit precisely, with a crack for leeway near the ceiling.

To permit a crack between the wall and floor means that you have to mount the section of wall in place elevated off the floor a half inch or so. This is accomplished by "hanging" the wall on heavy hinges as one would with any door. At the base of the wall section near the joining crack mount a heavy three-inch rubber caster. This will be hidden by the wall and the baseboard, but given quarter- or half-inch clearance, it will keep the hinged section from sagging with age. Now you can swing the section of wall open and closed. If your adjustments have been accurate, there will be a one-half-inch-or-so crack along the hinge side of the wall section. Now is the time to mount the last batten which will cover this joining, a removable batten affixed by one of the methods explained in the next chapter. Chapter 7 will also give you a method for making this wall section snap solidly in place when it is closed. Likewise, you will pick the method of attachment for the molding that runs along the ceiling and the baseboard. These too will be removable, but once snapped in place, the illusion of a solid and permanent wall is completed.

TRAPDOORS

Trapdoors are kind of dull. The ones you hear about are all alike. At best they are covered by a rug or a loud actor. I don't recommend such things. But, taking what you've learned here, you could invent some worthy designs. For example, small stairways can be built with concealed ropes and counterweights. Release your secret lock and you can lift the entire staircase, revealing another set of stairs going down into your secret basement. Another innovative trapdoor can be concealed under a seemingly permanent kitchen island. Release the lock and the counter slides to the side. I suspect you don't need any more idea encouragement along these lines. You are probably already ripping up mental floorboards.

SECOND SECRET ROOM

It occurs to me that you may be in the situation that makes a second secret room a plausible solution to your problem. One in one house, one in the other. Why not? Everybody's getting two of everything these days. Two dogs, two tractors, two degrees, two lovers, two drinks, two lines of defense, two children, two tickets, two putts, too much to do. Everything Chapter 5 says about secret-room construction applies here. In a small second home or cottage, it would be especially difficult to make a whole room forgotten. It doesn't take much smarts to see a square house on the outside, get inside, and wonder what ever happened to the back corner of the building.

If such a situation does face you, consider the basement, if you have one, or the one you will put in once you get turned on to the following idea. Basements have dirt behind their walls. Dirt can be dug out and secret rooms, like bomb shelters, root cellars, and misplaced septic tanks can be hidden right there on the other side of the basement wall.

Any of the wall ideas in this book that would provide a wide-enough entrance can serve as a door. The pilaster idea is eminently adaptable to basements. Wall-paneling approaches and movable shelf units likewise work well. I can imagine a dank basement in your old nineteenth-century farmhouse in the country. The walls are fieldstone, the floor dirt. And over on this wall an ancient cobwebbed shelf with who knows how old rotting preserves drawing attention to the dust. Wouldn't it be nice to grab that shelf in an inconspicuous place, pull it open, and walk into a brightly lit chamber, a storehouse for your secret compulsions. You can hide accordians there, go naked, sing loud, print salacious handbills. Yes, it brings a smile to my lips too.

Last Stop Before Special Appendix, Chapter 7

7
Fastening, Hinging, and Locking Devices

He fills, he bounds, connects, and equals all!
                                        —POPE

Hinges come in countless configurations.
There are different models for different functions and a never-ending parade of styles to satisfy the fickle customers of affluence. But just as hinges began simply with leather tacked to slabs of wood, there is no reason for us to obfuscate this issue more than is necessary. As far as secret building is concerned, there are two kinds of hinges, the visible and the invisible.

Visible hinges present an obvious problem; they can be seen when used as the fulcrum of the hidey hole. This can be overcome, fortunately, by covering the visible pivot of the hinge with a hollowed-out molding. Take the *Mellors Model*, for example. (See illustration.) There is no reason why you can't surround the backboard of the coatrack with miter-cut quarter-round molding. At the points where the hinges stick out, you chisel, carve, or rasp hollow areas in the molding to accommodate. Once it is secured in place, no one will be the wiser. The same technique can be used with secret compartments in any size. You will have to use larger moldings in many cases, of course, but if ·you buy those decorative molding strips, you will not only hide your hinge but enhance the beauty of your construct.

The basic styles you will want to consider for designs in this book are the heavy-duty hinge, the spring hinge, and the full-length hinge. The heavy-duty hinge can support heavy doors, large wall panels, and movable bookcases. The spring hinge like a dog has the loyal quality of always returning to place. When used with a *Secret Panel,* the spring inside the hinge will not only close the compartment for you once you are through fondling your privacies, but it can be installed out of sight at the back of the construct. The full-length hinge has very little visible fulcrum area, and this is correspondingly easy to conceal. You should familiarize yourself with each of these styles of hinge. Hold them in your hands. Talk to them. There is no reason to cut corners or costs when it comes to this stage of secret compartment building. It is the vital time.

Personally, I can find no more satisfactory hinge device than the invisible hinge. It not only serves the main purpose, but it does it with the élan of secrecy. The Soss hinge is an ingenious creation. If there is a Mr. Soss somewhere out there, I doff my hat and bow to you, Sir. This particular hinge is made in violent Detroit, Michigan, if you're interested in buying American. It comes in various sizes from teeny to hefty. Besides the wonderful look and feel of the Soss hinge, there is the totally engaging method in which it works. As it hinges open, the two sides separate along the fulcrum line. This is important because you avoid problems of friction and binding. When used with a *Spice Nook* or *Closet King,* the hung object doesn't rub against the wall as it swings out and open. Soss hinges are available from good hardware outlets everywhere.

Another invisible hinge, the *Hettich Kirchlengern* from West Germany, offers the same benefits as the Soss, is less expensive, but looks ugly. It does have one advantage and that is it snaps tightly into place when closed. It takes a strong tug to open it. Using this hinge in conjunction with cabinet fastener snaps, explained below, would give you such a tight closure that discovery would be next to impossible.

One minor drawback of the invisible hinges not always found with the conventional hinge is the necessity for mounting portions of them into the wood. This requires drilling and chiseling with exactitude. Good old Soss helps you with this problem though, giving you a template to trace around in preparing for installation. For a last-minute invisible hinge, see "Hinge" in Special Appendix.

Hinges

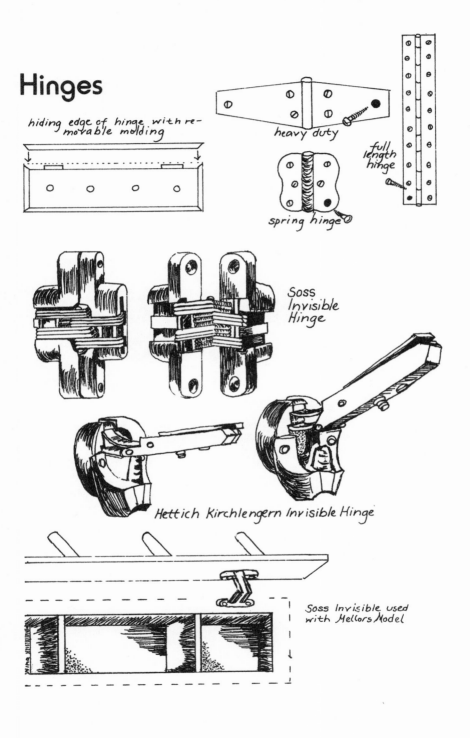

hiding edge of hinge with removable molding

heavy duty

full length hinge

spring hinge

Soss Invisible Hinge

Hettich Kirchlengern Invisible Hinge

Soss Invisible used with Mellors Model

When it comes to fastening an entrance over a secret compartment, you aren't required to use a hinge. Heavens to Betsy, no! In some cases, such as the *Book Basement*, a hinge won't work nearly as well as fastener snaps all around.

A great multipurpose fastening device is the common cabinet fastener friction snap. It consists of male and female sides. (See illustration.) One snaps inside the other, creating a strong connection. When used in series, as with the *Basic Baseboard*, or along one side of a *Gothic Wall* panel, there is no way a casual hand will discover it. To open your compartment merely takes a substantial pull. You can vary the difficulty here by increasing or decreasing the number of cabinet fasteners you use.

Another cabinet fastener is the magnet snap. It consists of a small magnet on one side and a metal plate on the other. One unit of these is not as strong as one unit of the friction snap. But again, used in series, you can determine how strong you want the adhesion between your solid member and the movable secret-compartment entrance. It comes in especially handy with smaller compartments such as the *Electric Outlet*, or the *Basic Baseboard*.

A grander refinement of this same magnet snap approach is to use larger horseshoe magnets in series. The illustration shows the simple process. Drill holes large enough to accommodate the magnet, then glue the magnets in place, making sure each face is perfectly aligned to snap against the metal plates that are attached to the movable member. There is no limit to the size of magnet you can use in this fashion. Very large magnets can serve you well in holding *Gothic Wall* panels in place. If you are interested in experimentation, see the heading "Magnets" in Special Appendix.

The simplest fastening method I know works well with small moldings and baseboards. Nail the unit in place using few nails. In the interim spaces place a few false nails. Now, pull the whole thing away from the wall. Careful prying may be necessary. Once it is in your hand, you can align the nails with their holes and push it back in place again, and repeat and repeat. The friction of the nails in their holes will keep the molding or baseboard looking solid in place. Wear and tear lessens efficiency so occasionally you will have to shim the holes with toothpicks or slivers of wood.

A few words about false nails and bolts. The concept is simple. With nails, cut off most of the length using a wire cutter. When you pound this in place in a molding, or bookshelf, it looks like a functioning nail. I'm a great believer in the proliferation of false nails in secret-compartment construction. Nothing throws sniffing creepers off the trail faster than a substantial-looking, multinailed structure.

You have to use a hacksaw to cut through bolts. The idea is the same. When you see a shiny bolt head and maybe a washer for a little extra class, you don't question the sturdiness of the attachment. You can use false bolts anywhere you think plausible.

I love Velcro. I love to hold the strips in my hands and pull them apart listening to them go crackle, crackle, then to push them back together again, never ceasing to wonder at modern science. Velcro strips are available from sewing centers and fabric and button stores everywhere. Velcro consists of two synthetic strips. One has a myriad number of tiny hooks. The other features an equal number of tiny loops. Press the two strips together and they catch and hold each other. Velcro is used in clothing instead of buttons and zippers. But there is no reason why you can't use it for hidey holes. It will do a dandy job holding electric plates in place, or moldings, or the baseboard. Glue the back of each Velcro strip to the parts that must lock together. You will have to experiment to determine just how much you should use for your particular job.

A handy method for opening closed panels and moldings is a pair of picks. They help you get enough purchase under slight edges of compartment access doors. With a pick it is easy to pull the hidey hole open. If you have acute fingernails or if you built your compartment so shabbily that there are large cracks to grasp, you might as well forget it. There are two varieties of what I call picks. One is made from ice picks. Cut off the bulk of the metal shaft, then sharpen the stub. This will give you greater leverage than the full length would permit, and it will also limit the damage your children can do if they dangerously assault one another. Another pick can be fashioned out of heavy gauge tin cut to four inches by six inches and mounted in a wood handle. This sort of pick disperses the force on the wood when the com-

Cabinet Fastener Friction Snap

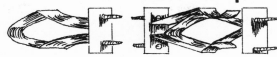

Cabinet Fastener Magnet Snap

Cabinet Fastener used with the Basic Baseboard.

etc.

Magnets

drill hole   magnet

glue magnet   metal plate

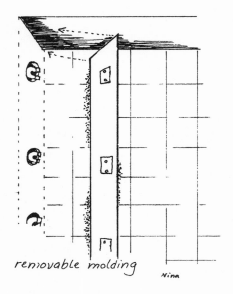

removable molding

Nina

False Nails

Picks

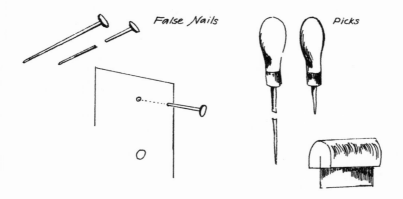

False Bolt with Washer Used with Spice Nook

Nail
Friction
Fastening

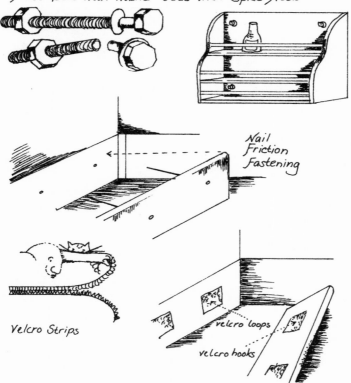

velcro loops

velcro hooks

Velcro Strips

Nina

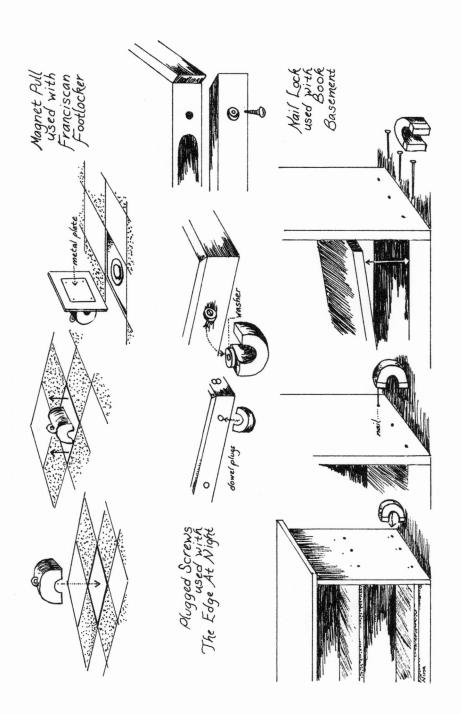

Magnet Pull used with Franciscan Footlocker

metal plate

Plugged Screws used with The Edge At Night

dowel plugs

washer

Nail Lock used with Book Basement

nail

partment door is especially difficult to open. My wife says forks make picks obsolete. You decide.

Magnets can be fun. Little pets for idle hands. They don't purr, wag their tails, or befoul the streets, but between your fingers they can create movement. They do have a life and a force of their own. In a way a magnet is a complex symbol reminding us of attraction, not repulsion, of nonfrigid poles, of the earth's spinning course through the firmament, of sibling stars and the real life-forces that pulse from galaxy to galaxy beyond our ken. A magnet is profound.

Is it any wonder, then, that a magnet can tap those mysterious life rhythms we all pigheadedly claim for our own province of understanding, and it transcends us to nonsectarian wisdom in our quest for more perfect secrecy. It is as if there were a magnet god somewhere saying, "I'll share my truth with you; here, have a magnet." Use it to sooth your anxieties by secretly locking your insecurity. All we can say is thank you, Big Magnet, for this uncommon gift—a magnet release for secret compartments.

The *Magnet Pull* is simplicity itself, as in atom or cell. For example, with the *Franciscan Footlocker* there is a problem of lifting the parquet wood square or the selected floor tile. A pick can be used, but after a time there is the danger of wear and tear at the edge which will call attention to the hiding place. If you glue a metal plate to the back of the chosen square section, however, all you need do is place a large magnet at the top, then praise be and, presto, the compartment is opened unto you. The same technique can be adapted to a secret panel, *Electric Outlet Subterfuge,* or any of a number of other compartment designs.

A similar approach that works well with the *Edge at Night* hidey hole is *Plugged Screws.* A commonly used and very attractive technique in furniture construction has wood screws in sunken holes holding it all together. (See illustration.) These are hidden by dowels the same size as the drilled holes, cut and sanded to be flush with the outer surface. Attractive circles of wood thus highlight and accentuate an otherwise bland plane of wood. With the *Edge at Night,* the sunken screws can hold the molding in place, and the dowel plugs can have a metal washer glued to their inside end. Once pushed into the hole over the screw, the dowel looks permanent. But along comes a magnet and whiz, the metal washer is attracted, popping the dowel plug out of the hole.

A magnet-locking technique that I have used frequently is the *Nail Lock*. Take the *Book Basement* as an example. Narrow-headed finish nails are often used with bookshelves. They are pounded in from the ends as is shown in the illustration. No one would consider such nails removable. But that is just what happens with the *Nail Lock*. Using an electric drill, prepare holes for the nails, slightly larger than the nails themselves. Push the nails in place by hand and the construct looks permanently affixed. Indeed, the shelf/door to the *Book Basement* is secured in place. Stop playing with your magnet and bring it to bear; quick as a quirk, the nails speed from their mountings, releasing your door to the secret compartment.

The *Nail Lock* can be adapted for use with many secret compartments. The placement of finish nails is not questioned if they appear in some regular pattern. A *Nail Lock* from one side is a simple matter to add to *False Corner Furring*. When using it with more difficult constructions such as the *Spice Nook*, you must hollow out a small female hole in the back so that a male protrusion of wood affixed to the wall will fit into it when the spice rack is closed into place. A *Nail Lock* can then be inserted from the side of the spice rack, intercepting the male protrusion inside the hollowed-out hole, thus locking the *Spice Nook* in place.

It is time to speak out for glue. A purist would never consider using anything less than nails or screws for fastening hardware. But there are times when it is easier to use durable epoxy glue or paste to affix a hinge, especially when access for nailing and screwing is limited. Epoxy will hold just as well as screws, and it harkens back to the kinds of satisfaction you found as a child pasting blue bunnies on your kindergarten class project mural. There is one cautionary note to be inserted here, however. If your alignment is ill-conceived, or should some other unforeseen problem arise, you could be faced with a permanently connected monstrosity. It takes confidence to use glue. But, as George Washington said, hatchet in hand, "It takes confidence to do anything well."

Here Comes Special Appendix

Special Appendix

Idleness is an appendix to nobility.
—BURTON

Affair, How to Hide an Affair: I stood on New York's East Fiftieth Street once, stretching my legs after several hours of taxi driving. A long, low, quiet, fish-gray Cadillac pulled up across the street. A pale white bald head of an old fat man was straining to see through the steering wheel as he stopped by a hydrant. An uptown call girl, young and beautiful, stacked on red platform shoes, stepped from the shadow of the building and entered the limousine. He must have given the chauffeur the day off and now he was jerkily driving toward some secret destination with his beauty. I would not recommend this approach to hiding an affair. Clearly inferior. Rather, I would first ask the cogent question, "Why is an affair necessary?" Failing a response, I would then recommend the following approaches to love trysting. Do it out of town if possible. Be as brief as you can about it. You have to consider every ramification of your actions. Anticipation is the shrewdest cloak of secrecy. If possible, first undertake a six-month training period in which you practice lying to your family, each member. When you're ready, don't be surprised if you get taken over. Old Demon Love got you. Try to get a job with a corporation in South America. (See *Corporation.*) Also consider disappearing for a while, either cold turkey or ostensibly to do a special agent chore for the CIA. The Fatherland my Fatherland. (See also *Yourself*, How to Hide Yourself.) When you feel it getting out of your system, place a long-distance call and go home. What if he or she follows you back home? Peering in your windows after dinner when the children can see. Special ingenuity is needed with these sorts of situations. Find unusual places to meet. Like the zoo or the aquarium. Take hand-holding walks along railroad tracks among the weeds or in parked railroad cars where you can pitch woo. Big-building elevators can be taken over and parked inconspicuously between floors at the sub-level if you buy a key from a Maintenance Man. Use lunch hours. Also get in the habit of "going to work early." Steal money slowly from the bank accounts for presents and expenses. Do special favors at work to get flexibility in your work schedule. Buy a panel truck or van so you can use every minute available to you. Park in huge employee parking fields around factories in the daytime, a rural spot with trees and trickling water at night. Always have a fail-safe story to tell. Never have an affair with a crazy person.

Air-Conditioner, Secret Compartment Inside Air-Conditioner: In general it isn't a good idea to make a secret place inside an electrical appliance. These are often the first victims of thievery. The air-conditioner however, isn't easily carted off, and is usually shunned by all but the most robust of rogues. Consequently, it is a wonderful source of ample hiding space. Remove the face from the machine, pull out the air-conditioning unit and discard. You are left with the empty shell, like a locust. After hiding something, put the face back on, making sure buttons and knobs still appear in place.

Auto Hidey Hole, A Compartment in Your Car: We all can't afford those sporty cars with the center console, even though we pride our vehicles like we take our women. But if a tight little sporty console is what you want to get into, you can build one that fits between your legs and your wife's, over the transmission hump. It could solve that nagging problem, where to mount the stereo tape deck so it won't be ripped off by tensed hands in the high crime time. (See illustration.) Stuff the magnet up under the dash when not using it to open the nail lock.

Auto
Hidey Hole

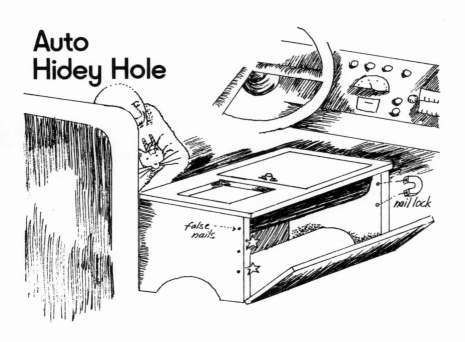

nail lock

false nails

Tools

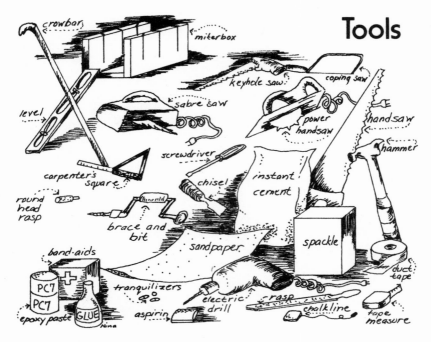

crowbar

miterbox

keyhole saw

coping saw

sabre saw

level

power handsaw

handsaw

screwdriver

hammer

carpenter's square

chisel

instant cement

round head rasp

brace and bit

sandpaper

spackle

band-aids

PC7

PC7

tranquilizers

duct tape

epoxy paste

GLUE

aspirin

electric drill

rasp

chalkline

tape measure

Automobile, How to Hide an Automobile: There are professional car thieves and then the car-thief hobbiests. Both can be thwarted by humility—owning a car that is several years old, of an undistinguished make, preferably shabby on the exterior—in short, one which stands out about as much as a parking meter. America is still a country of trees, bark, and leaves. Paint your car a pastel earth color. The more you look like nature intended you, the more invisible you'll be. Automobiles are so common these days, you can park one anywhere, even among trees in the country, and it will quickly assume the character of junk. Something people walk around, grateful that they don't have to dodge it. (See also *Garage.*)

Camouflage, Principles of Camouflage: First put your secret in a little frequented area. Think of zebras. They don't stand in roadways waiting for tour buses. They're in the thickets. Next, adorn, paint, and cover your object so that it looks as much like its background as possible. Solid colors do not exist in nature's landscape. Broken color patterns and dark spots to simulate voids are the tricks of the outdoor camoufleur. Often war surplus and mail order outlets have camouflage netting and clothing. There's nothing as much fun as sitting in the woods wearing camouflaged coveralls and hat with a mud-smeared face, chortling while your family beats the bushes looking for you. One mail order outfit handling Government Surplus items is Airborne Sales Co., 8501 Steller Drive, Box 2727, Culver City, California 90230. Fifty cents for a catalog.

Carpentry. Discourse on Carpentry Tools and Skills: It is not my intention to train neophytes into competent carpenters. There are books published toward this end already. Among them: *The Practical Handbook of Carpentry.* An expert takes the novice from basic workshop to building a frame house. Topics covered include: buying lumber, use of tools, installing built-ins, and building furniture. Available for $2.25 from Fawcett Publications, Fawcett Place, Greenwich, Connecticut 06830. If you have a lot of money, consider the four-volume *Carpenters and Builders Library.* Everything is covered here for $18.50 from Theodore Audel & Co., 4300 West Sixty-second Street, Indianapolis, Indiana 46268. None of this is really necessary if you are brave of heart and willing to accept new challenges and smashed thumbs, frustration as well as fulfillment. You will find that putting things together with your hands is merely process, learned in the main by doing. Take a hammer in your hand, immediately you know what to do with it. Take a handsaw, practice cutting straight lines, watching out for your left hand. I have a scar between my first and second knuckles dating back to age eight and my first efforts at using a saw. Don't mess with an electric circular saw until your muscles are stronger and you have gained competence with hand tools. A keyhole saw is manual, being a narrow blade that can fit into a drilled hole. It permits you to cut holes in the floor, in a counter top or what-have-you, the same thing that an electric saber saw will do much more easily. A coping saw cuts in all directions, as in a jigsaw puzzle. Just as with business, chiseling is quickly learned as a useful method for opening space in walls, cement floors, or in a board for hinges or fasteners. No one needs to tell you about crowbars. A brace and bit is a joy to use. It's simple. You put pressure on the top and crank it around and you've drilled a hole. An electric drill will make smaller holes fast. The humming sound is an aesthetic pleasure all its own. A round head rasp works quickly in paring off quantities of wood when used mounted in an electric drill. If you can't use a screwdriver, return to high school and take "Shop." A tape measure does a better job than guessing. For cutting boards at perfect 90-degree angles, use a carpenter's square. Again, once the tool is in your hand, common sense tells you how to proceed. A miter box permits cuts of 45 degrees. A chalk line can be handy in making straight lines over long distances. You pull the string from the chamber and stretch it taut between two distant points. Raise the string up with one hand, increasing the tension, and when you release it, it will snap back against the surface, leaving a nice baby-blue line of chalk. A level is nothing more than a captured bubble. When you get the bubble perfectly aligned, the level is level. Understand? I have a fondness for the new super glues. They are quick and easy to use, exceedingly strong and cheap. PC-7 epoxy paste is a favorite. Duct tape can come in handy at the most surprising times. It is a durable heavy cloth tape. If you want to take the easy way out, loops of this tape will hold moldings in place for short duration. It's the kind of tape that kidnappers use over victims' mouths. For people who really want to learn what they are doing, there are courses offered in adult

Hiding A House

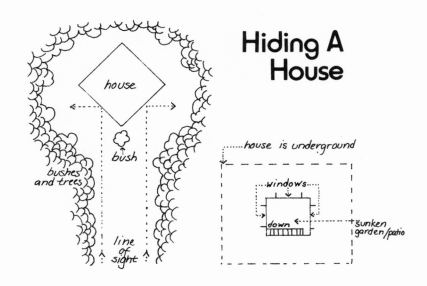

house

bush

bushes
and trees

line
of
sight

house is underground

windows

down

sunken
garden/patio

Hollow Leg

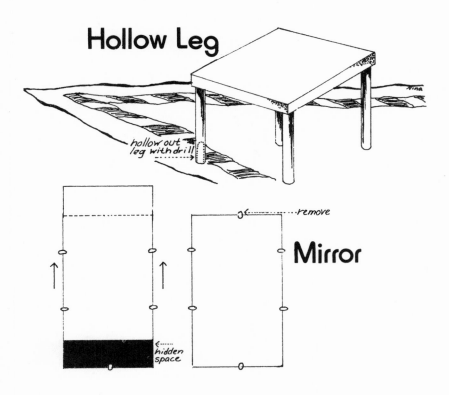

hollow out
leg with drill

remove

Mirror

hidden
space

education programs everywhere. But think of our forefathers. They didn't know anything. Most of them were thieves sprung to a hostile continent; what did they know about carpentry? You too can start with basics. Practice on unambitious projects, and soon you'll be dreaming of building a house in the woods and hunting turkeys.

Ceiling, How to Make a False Closet Ceiling: Cut a piece of three-quarter-inch plywood the same size as the ceiling. Nail moldings in place around the four walls six inches or a foot down from the actual ceiling. The plywood section will rest on top of these, acting as if it belongs there. Push up to reach your space. Primed and painted like the rest of the closet, it will fool some of the people all of the time.

Chimney, Creating a False Tin Chimney: Instant fireplaces are popular these days, as are frozen entrees at the best restaurants, plastic money, and indefensible movies. For the more pure of heart, there are Franklin stoves which, like those conical tin fireplaces, make use of segments of tin flues for the chimney. These are at home in wilderness cabins as well as in posh modern residences. It is an easy matter to run the real tin chimney concealed inside a wall, while a fake one is visible in the room. This technique can be utilized most easily on the second floor where the transition from downstairs to upstairs can hide your main-line diversion. To reach the ample hidden space in the false chimney only requires pulling one segment loose.

Corporation, How to Hide in a Corporation: Nothing could be easier. There is no character in mass identity. Therefore we are getting less character to worry about these days. Seen, stamped out. If being different bothers you, being noticed, talked about, or talked to, give up your cares and meld with a corporation. Start at the bottom if you have to. There's nowhere to go but up. It is a bit like heaven. Clean and antiseptic inside, your dirt inconspicuously scattered worldwide like the memories of populist assassinations. The smarter you are, the more fun you can have. You can't imagine the things that can be hidden in computers.

Dead Space, Using Dead Space for Concealment: Many buildings, especially apartments, have areas of dead space built

into them to accommodate plumbing, vents, or whimsical archi-
tects. If you can locate such spaces, either through blueprints,
hearsay, or measurement and observation, you can break through
a wall to find a lot of room for a hidey hole and hopefully not
your neighbor's screaming wife. The secondary attachment you
employ to cover the hole should, as always, be plausible and
tasteful.

Desk, Daring Desk Top Secret Compartment: America grows
not in the farmer's fields all flaxen and fertilized, nor in the factories, tall stacked and din filled, but rather in the offices at the
desks. Desks make America great, and here is one of the best
ideas for desk concealment that has ever come down the turn-
pike. Take the top of your desk off, hinge one side with Soss
hinges, use a secret-locking device on the other, and you will have
a bureaucratic breadth of hidden space available right under your
nose.

Frontispiece, Enumeration of the 17 Secret Compartments
in the Frontispiece Illustration: the Mellors Model, Electric Out-
let Subterfuge, the Franciscan Footlocker, Elementary Secret
Panel, the Edge at Night, the Basic Baseboard, In the Baby
Moose Head (see *Gargoyles*), Hollowed Leg, Hinged Book-
shelves Hiding a Room, the Plato Panel, the Wood Pile, Pilaster,
False Corner Furring, Surreptitious Sill, Door Jamb Safe, the
Kicker, and Footstooling.

Garage, How to Hide Things in the Garage: If the wall studs
of your garage are lined with plywood, plasterboard, or some
other covering, you can employ many of the previously discussed
secret compartments there (e.g., the *Mellors Model*). If not,
consider hiding things in the dark inaccessible eaves. You can
use a long pole with a hook at the end for placement and retrieval
of a secret box painted black. You might also consider mounting
that heavy forbidding-looking workbench on shielded casters so
that at night you can push it out of the way by flashlight glow
and reach what is hidden in the floor under it. If your garage is
mounted into a hillside, with the back wall abutted against dirt,
consider making a secret room behind a *Wall Storehousing* board
and batten paneled wall. You could even park the car in there if
you fear for its safety.

Gargoyles, Gargoyles, Stuffed Animal Heads and the Like: If your wall is ornamented with a mounted fish, stuffed deer head, moose, or any other gargoyle-like object, consider making a secret compartment in it. I even saw a stuffed pinto head in a department store once (Gertz, East Hampton, New York). Ideally, a taxidermist can be found to conspire with you in devising an entrance device, possibly a heavy-duty spring hinge to hold the head tight against its wood mounting board. Or maybe you'll be able to poke the bear's eye to make the mouth open. You can always use a flap of hairy skin and Velcro.

Hinge, Last-Minute Invisible Hinge: Lucky you! A last minute invisible hinge has come to my attention. It is a beautiful cylinder hinge for 180-degree openings, made of profile brass. I wish I knew about this one sooner. You can get them from SISO Export Ltd., 26 NYROPGade, 1602 Copenhagen, Denmark.

House, How to Hide a House: Short of encasing it in a false factory building, the most viable approach to house hiding is the one utilizing nature's forest setting. Start from scratch and build a modern square house with a flat roof. Instead of normal frame construction, employ glass panels, floor to ceiling, to cover the entire exterior. Use the newly developed insulated glass with reflective properties from one side and see-through clarity from the other. In effect, this sort of glass is a one-way mirror, and is energy conserving according to its manufacturer. Libby-Owens-Ford Company, 811 Madison Avenue, Toledo, Ohio 43695, makes Vari-Tran, a reflective glass often found in skyscrapers as well as modern homes. PPG Industries of Pittsburgh makes a similar product. Design your house to contain as much glass and as little visible framing structure as possible. The ideal location to make such a house disappear into the setting is a keyhole-shaped clearing in the forest. The only cleared approach to the house is from the bottom of the keyhole toward the circle clearing in which the house is built diagonal to the line of sight. (*See illustration.*) Plant a fir or spruce tree to cover the visible corner vertical of the house. Anyone looking up that leaf-strewn path would see only forest and reflection of forest. You will be hidden safely in your successful illusion. Another, slightly more elaborate, approach to house concealment is to build it completely underground. Leave an ample open patio pit in the center.

This will permit a window wall for each room. Completely invisible until you are standing above the patio looking down into it, you'll descend the steps into your sunken courtyard with the élan of a deer, knowing the only intruders to fear are the animals that will fall in breaking their necks right by your kitchen cooking pot.

Legs, Hollowed-Out Legs: This secret compartment dates back as far as inanimate legs, a recommendation and a drawback. Banal and easy, it still gets the job done. Legs of chairs, tables, orthopedic legs, you name it. If you ever have a lot of money to transport, try this trick. Put on welfare clothes and one shoe (remember your immigrant genes), drill a hole in the end of one crutch, insert your money in very large bills, replace the rubber crutch tip and hobble to your rendezvous.

Magnets, Sources of Magnets: I would recommend your buying magnets from hardware outlets so you can see and test what you're buying. But if you're snowbound in Montana or for some other reason want to order through the mail, consider these sources: Edmund Scientific Co. advertises 3½- and 1½-pound horseshoe magnets, war surplus. The larger one, they claim, lifts forty pounds on land, more if dredging the bottom of your polluted river. The large one is $11.50 and the smaller $6.50. Send for their free catalog at 300 Edscorp Building, Barrington, New Jersey 08007. Ask for "Free Giant Catalog 'C'." A less impressive source, a Mr. Magnet, resides at 90 Harold Lane, Paradise, California 95969, and advertises twenty disc magnets for $1.00, twenty assorted metal and ceramic for $2.00, and thirty-five assorted magnets for $3.00.

Mirror, Secret Compartment Behind a Mirror: This arrangement works well with full-length mirrors mounted on the wall or on a door. Use those little mirror-holding tabs available at hardware stores. (*See illustration.*) All you have to do to get at the secret space is to remove the top tab and slide the mirror up.

Money, Hiding Money on Your Person: Here's a little trick I first learned from a world traveler in Africa. He was following the ancient trade routes around the world for the second time, and he had yet to lose his money, which he always carried in

Outdoor Hidey Holes

dead bush

fake hornet's nest

under rock

bottom of fallen log

under bird bath

Slick Sliding Panel used with Plato Panel

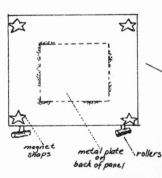

magnet snaps

metal plate on back of panel

rollers

slide and pull magnet to close

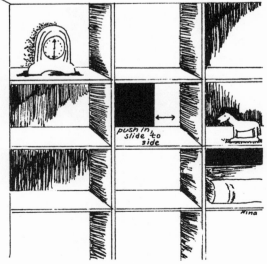

push in to slide to side

Nina

cash. He had a normal-looking good quality belt made of two pieces of leather stitched together along the edges. On the inside of the belt, he had slit the leather and installed a zipper. A simple, functional secret place for large bills. You can do the same thing yourself, or you can order one ready-made. Big Three Enterprises calls it "Safeguard Money-Saver" and it costs $3.00, ordered from 34 Garfield Place, Brooklyn, New York 11215. State size, 28-44, and color, brown or black. A less expensive approach is to roll your money up into a tight tube, insert it into a cheap plastic ball-point pen. Carry it in some out-of-the-way place so no one will be tempted to borrow it.

Mouth, Hiding Things in the Mouth: The quintessential hidey hole is the mouth. Caught by surprise, you can cast small compromising objects into it. Out of the way to the side of your mouth, you'll be able to feign normalcy, say little and head for the bathroom. Truly the grandest orifice, the mouth is always ready for service, to devour, to nuzzle, to smile, or to hide the truth away.

Nation, How to Hide an Old Nation: If you've stayed with me this far, I'm going to discuss something I don't share with just anyone. That is, the power potential of our national secrecy. We have the power to be very secret as a nation. If you are secret and I am secret, then we are secret. And if two and two and fifty make a million, we'll see that day come round. Now, what would happen if we agreed to keep just one fault, our worst, a secret? For example, the rapist who doesn't let *anyone* know. The lucre manipulator who, to keep his compulsion secret, exiles himself to a multinational corporation plantation in South America. You can imagine the contortions some lives would go through, should some of us accept the challenge, should we be selfless to this extent in our dedication to the Republic. If one percent of the population in a period of ten years joined *The Corps Of Secrecy,* crime would be crushed, smiles buffed, religious fervor and our feathered eagle fluffed, the nation, in short, saved.

Nervousness, How to Hide Timorousness: Read the book, *Creative Aggression* by Dr. George R. Bach and Dr. Herb Goldberg, available from Doubleday & Co., Inc., publishers, for $8.95. Here you will learn what travesties have been visited upon your head by the myth of "niceness." You will also learn how to break through to those vital juices stewing in your stomach. A cheap alternative is *The Art Of Selfishness* by David Seabury, a Pocket Books paperback for $1.25. First published in 1937, the reasons for its longevity are obvious.

On Hiding Things, Examination of the Phenomenon: Have you ever noticed the shifty-eyed people around you? How they are always hiding parts of themselves? An aunt hides her hands under tables and lace. A neighbor hides terror behind a shoe-salesman optimism. There are those who hide their insecurity in the safety of decorum, hushing noises so the world will appear as silent as a Kleenex. It is no small wonder then that people like these are likely to hide other, more nasty traits. If you knew where to look, you could find rigid-faced men storing guns, grenades, mortars, and ammo, a preparation for the fight against time and those who represent it. You can find husbands cheating at hearts, and wives hiding the good booze so "he don't drink it." There are people who are hiding their anger at their lives behind bovine eyes, who hide in bars concealing the fact their only security is a blue blanket of light and the wet *oui oui* of false camaraderie. Obviously, the solution to all of this is to do away with the necessities for hiding. But that is like praying for freedom and justice for all. My personal solution is to be as unto camouflage and hide with style. We can at least be unique in that.

Outside, Hiding Things out of Doors: Take one of those foot-high hornets' nests like they have in high school laboratories stuck up on a shelf collecting dust. Hollow out an entrance from the top, put your privacies in there, then hang it high in an easy climbing tree. No one will approach it. Hollow out a secret compartment on the underside of a fallen log in the forest. Make a trap door under a dead bush. The cracks can be obscured by an ample layer of musky leaves. Underneath the trapdoor can be a small burrow or a whole chamber. Perform a similar number on your birdbath. The birds don't mind as long as you keep putting water in the dish top. A good hiding place for a short duration is under a large rock in a stream. Not recommended in the spring rainy season when your secret could surface like a Mafia corpse.

Wall Expansion

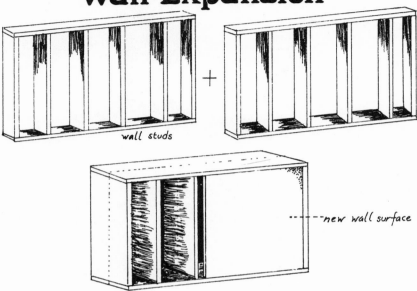

wall studs

+

new wall surface

Rustic Walls

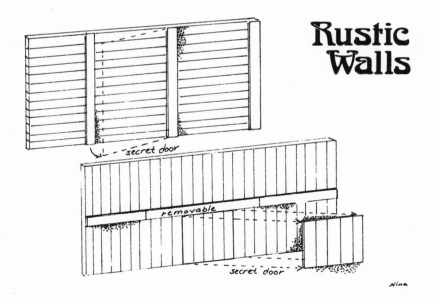

secret door

removable

secret door

Nina

Plants, Flower Pot Secret Compartment: Take a large flower pot and make a removable bottom for it. Inside the pot creating a two-inch dead space at the base, construct a new bottom to hold the weight of dirt and roots. A hole with a rubber tube should be fashioned and epoxy pasted in place to allow water runoff to pass through the secret compartment below. Now, plant an asparagus fern or some other bushy plant to shroud the pot in foliage. With a house full of plants, this is excellent concealment.

Retribution, Secret Compartments with Traps: Nothing is more natural than wanting to get even. The Bible teaches us that, as well as the opposite. But should you consider punishing your burglar by building a hand-severing trap inside your hidey hole, pause for the following. I grew up in America's heartland, a postage-stamp American. One day I discovered I was the latest victim of the finger burglar. He had taken seven sweat-stained dollars from my high school baseball locker-hung trousers. I had been busting my buns on the practice field for the team, for the school, for the nuns even, only to be visited with this indignation. I scratched my flat top and conspired. The device I chose was calculated not only to catch the villain, but to brand him with guilt and exact punishment all at one stroke. It was a mousetrap affixed to an old wallet. On the trap jaw, I soldered half-inch-long pin ends. All the thieving coward had to do was sandwich his hand around my wallet again, and he would find his fingers run through. He would be easy to pick out of the school body the next day. Maybe there would even be a trail of blood from the locker room to his house. I am now proud to say I never executed the plan. The blond, blue-eyed fatherless youth was captured by other means.

Rustic Walls, Another Approach to Paneling: If you want something a bit more crude than the *Gothic Wall, Board and Battens,* or *Wall Paneling,* one of these rustic approaches may be right for you. (*See illustration.*) You may choose the vertical or horizontal board treatment. Boards from old farm outbuildings are especially attractive utilized this way. The wall is paneled with boards cut to equal length. Perpendicular boards are nailed to cover the junction cracks. Because the junction cracks of the boards are covered in this way, it is an easy matter to create a secret door in a similar fashion to that explained in Chapter 6, *Wall Storehousing*.

Slick Sliding Panel, A Better Class of Plato Panel: Refresh your memory of the *Plato Panel*, then consider this. Install four or more magnet snaps at the corners of the *face* side of a slightly oversized panel. (*See illustration*.) This will permit the panel to snap firmly in place against the back of the bookcase. Mount a large metal plate in the middle of the backside of the panel. Attach two rollers or small casters to the bottom of the panel. Then at the bottom of the opening of the bookcase, mount a wood strip to act as a track for the panel to slide along to the side. To open it, once the panel is in place, simply push back, breaking the connection of magnets and slide the panel to the side, revealing the hidden space you've opened there. To close the panel, slide it back in position, using a large magnet applied to the center of the panel to draw it toward you, making it snap into place.

Tools, Sources for Tools: If you know what you're buying by familiarity with brand names and tool types, mail order is fine. Otherwise, stick to your local hardware store. For $1.00 you can get the 196-page Silvo Hardware Co. Tool Catalog from 107 Walnut Street, Philadelphia, Pennsylvania 19106.

Wall Expansion, Deeper Space Between Wall Studs: If you are building a secret compartment utilizing the dead space between wall studs but would like more depth to the space, you can expand the wall in the following manner. Construct a new wall frame, mounting the studs exactly as they are in the original wall. (*See illustration*.) Once this wall frame is juxtaposed to the original, you will have twice the depth available for your compartment. If it can be plausibly done without drawing attention to the depth discrepancy, you can increase the depth of the wall by more than one factor. Unfortunately, you will have to recover the entire surface you have constructed. Be it plaster or paneling, you must make the new wall look exactly like the others. This technique is especially suited to the end walls in rectangular rooms.

Window Seat, A Sunlit Secret Place: Everyone loves a window seat. Romance can be kindled there, or you can while away hours on your window-seat cushion, watching your neighbors through binoculars. Seats can be constructed in bay windows, or in front of normal sash types. If there is an obvious space concealed under the seat cushion of your design, it certainly won't be an inconspicuous place. But you can make an obvious storage area under the seat and then at the very bottom a small secret place similar in design to the *Book Basement*. Some window seats cover radiators or air-conditioning units. In and around such items, you will have an easy time constructing a hiding nook. Window seats are a suitable backlit pedestal for women. They're a great place to sing from, cascading melodies out into your flowered bowers. Or, if you happen to be important, you can appear there, looking down on the people looking up at you.

Woodworkers, Sources of Materials: If you don't live in an area blessed with quality wood and lumber outlets, consider sending for these catalogs. They offer imported hardwoods, veneers, carving woods, moldings, kits and plans along with hard-to-find hardware. Each catalog is fifty cents. Woodworkers Catalog from Constantine, 2053 Eastchester Road, Bronx, New York 10461. Craftsman Catalog from Craftsman, 2729 Mary, Chicago, Illinois 60608.

Yourself, How to Hide Yourself: As a general approach, try to dress like everyone else. Wear the kinds of glasses they do. Pay to have your hair fixed according to the current fashion. Don't limp, have scars, or smell funny. To be more specific: contact your local organized crime representative and buy new identity papers, travel to a large city at least a thousand miles away, and get a job that you hate. The expression of frustration and despair on your face will keep friendly busybodies at a distance. If possible, go out in public only at night. Avoid neighborhoods where police hassle people. From my own experience, I can heartily recommend working at night as a janitor, the silent invisible service of cleaner-uppers, who sing only to themselves, "Nobody knows the rubble we clean. Nobody knows or sees us."

THE END

CREDITS

I am very grateful for the contributions of the following:

Illustrator: Nina Sklansky
Editor: Robert Levine
Editorial Advice: Narcisse Chamberlain
Literary Agent: Elaine Markson
Copy Editor: Elizabeth K. Lieberman
Jacket Designers: George Romero and Nina Sklansky